The SAF®

For us

Part One::
SAF®
Technology
& Infrared Scans

Part Two:
The Guide to SAF® Online
Finding Interpretations & Remedies

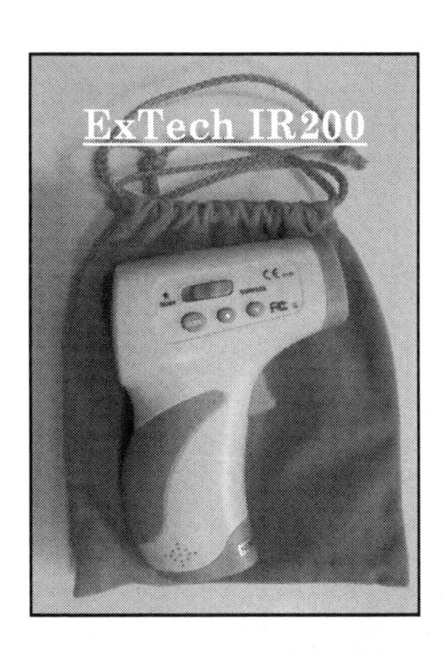

Kathy M. Scogna
Joseph R. Scogna, Jr.

The SAF® Infrared Manual

(for use with the ExTech IR 200)

Part One: SAF® Technology & Infrared Scans
Part Two: The Guide to SAF® Online

Published by Kathy M. Scogna - www.LifeEnergyResearch.com
www.KathyScogna.com (Interviews and more Books)

NOTE: This work reflects the research of Joseph R. Scogna, Jr. as found in his books, manuals, seminars, and computer programs. This is not a medical manual nor should it be used to diagnose disease or to prescribe drugs. The information is presented here for those who want to help themselves and others understand their life more fully and make informed holistic decisions about their health.

Remember, our health, wellness and lifestyle choices are and have always been our own responsibility. The reader is urged to evaluate his or her health status and if disease, poor health, illness, or continuing symptoms of any sort are present, he or she is urged to seek a health practitioner.

ISBN-13: 978-1500130091 (CreateSpace-Assigned)
ISBN-10: 1500130095

SAF® Infrared Manual
includes index
1. infrared scans 2. holistic interpretations 3. energetic healing 4. Self Awareness Formulas (SAF®) 5. SAF® Online

I. Kathy M. Scogna, author II. Joseph R. Scogna, Jr. author
III. title

Table of Contents

Foreword–Infrared Upgrade

In Joe Scogna's day, as many of you have seen on You-Tube videos, the Infrared Sensitizer and the Apple IIe computer were one dynamic machine. Apple computers were king then; IBM had yet to create the PC (personal computer) and very few people or practitioners had a computer or even saw the need for one.

Joe had worked with several devices and then found a suitable infrared device he could incorporate as part of his system; data would enter his SAF® computing system and be tabulated into a sequence of numbers. Once created, the sequence was interpreted as to the stressed emotions, organs and glands, and then remedies were found with various computer programs. It was all cutting edge; it did what he had envisioned, and then some.

Fast forward to the 21st century! My, how times have changed. When we decided it was time to upgrade, what type of computer should we choose – a PC or Mac? Microsoft or Linux? Would it work in Europe, South America, Australia, and Asia? And finally, does today's busy practitioner even <u>want</u> another computer to clutter the office?

Jezra, our resident programmer, came up with the idea of an online system so that ANYONE in any country around the world, who had access to the Internet, could use it. And we would make it cost effective so practitioners, researchers, and students could afford it. Three questionnaires were the initial intake for chain creation while we hunted for an appropriate infrared device.

We found it! The handheld ExTech IR 200 is perfect — it is inexpensive, easy to use and portable, so no USB to tether us to a chair or office. The unit stores the temperature values in memory so we can be mobile and scan children, the elderly, even animals (read *Joe Scogna, SAF® and the Horse*, page 47). The values can be entered immediately into your SAF® Online account, or entered later on from any location with Internet access.

With this new infrared Sensitizer, there are no separate computer programs to purchase because these are built into the SAF® Online database (see The Guide to SAF® Online starting on page 55).

Armed with the IR 200, you will simply follow the instructions and the Gravinometric Face Points in this book (Cover illustration and pgs. 17-21).

In less than a minute, the scan will be complete, you will enter the data, and you are ready to decipher the chain sequence for your client.

And that is the point, isn't it? To help your clients and participants find relief from their most pressing issues, to help them follow the emotion clues, to resolve emotional conflicts and to increase their vibration level.

As the Hippocratic Oath states:

"I will give no deadly medicine to any one.
I will prescribe regimens for the good of my patients according to my ability and my judgment and never do harm to anyone."

With the IR 200 and SAF® Online, you have a tool that works consistently in these challenging times, and one that adheres to the Hippocratic oath. The SAF® Online computing system is the hope and the method needed for our transformation.

We are excited about this latest addition to SAF® — it is still cutting edge! This completes the computing upgrade and brings full circle the life energy work of Joe Scogna—we are now ready to help a new generation.

Join us!

—Kathy M Scogna
2013
www.KathyScogna.com

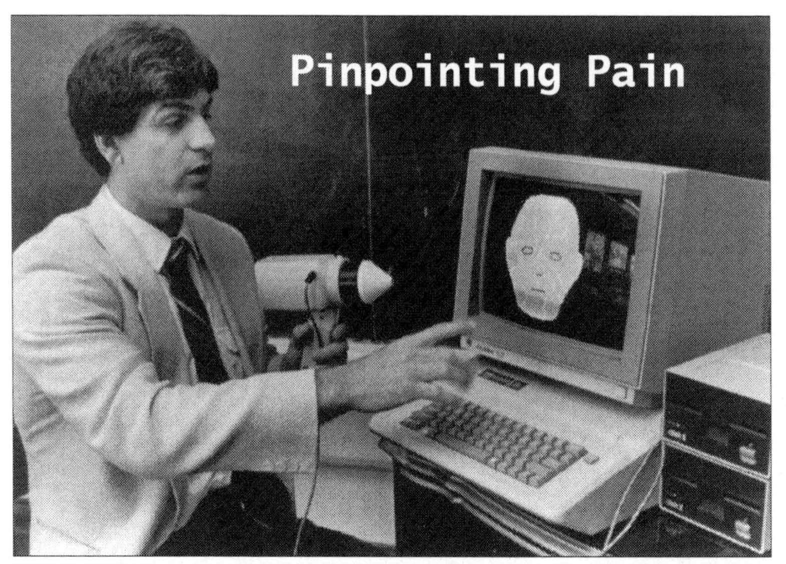

Pinpointing Pain

Joseph R. Scogna, Jr., demonstrating the Infrared Sensitizer and the Life Energy Computer System, 1986

by Annette Damato, Reading Eagle Times (excerpt)

Joseph R. Scogna, Jr. may be on the threshold of futuristic medicine by revising and revitalizing some of the practices of ancient medicine.

Scogna, owner and director of Life Energy Foundation Inc, has combined the technology of computer electronics with the wisdom of the ages to pinpoint not only exactly what ails a person, but why.

"The kind of ailment you don't often hear about, those are the things we look for and address," said Scogna, who studied university physics and chemistry. "The little quirks of pain, the type of ailment for which a doctor will give you a Valium."

"We believe the pains people feel are efforts of the body trying to communicate to people. Pain is simply your body trying to speak, trying to communicate a source of trouble."

"Through infrared patterns, we believe we can translate those symptoms. Instead of taking an aspirin trying to cover up a pain, a person should be trying to find the source of it. By covering up the source of the pain with medication, the communication circuits are numbed and the message cannot come through."

By using an infrared sensitizer, similar to a device that detects steam trapped in pipes by monitoring heat changes, Scogna can detect heat changes in the body.

"A heat change may indicate a changing condition in a specific part of the body. Every emotion, every ailment, has a complex logarithmic statement. For instance, the sequence of numbers 1-22 indicate a bone disorder; 16-20 indicates Bright's Disease (a kidney disorder); and a 4-23 in the middle of the logarithmic chain indicates a food allergy. When we see 14-17/18, the person is building up fat cells for protection, and a 13-20 is depression."

"In some ways it sounds as if we're Ghostbusters," Scogna said. "But this is very logical. It's body talk, and body talk is basically the expression of the body when it is in trouble."

The people who want to be assessed are not crazy.

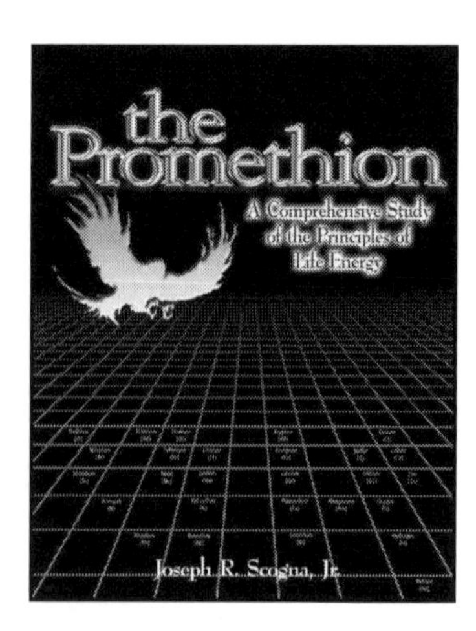

In *The Promethion: A Comprehensive Study of the Principles of Life Energy*, Scogna reunites spiritual alchemy with physical chemistry/alchemy as he traces history and personality of the elements combined with a catalog of environmental chemicals, their effects, and their antidotes.

The elements are presented from an energetic stance. How to balance the electric pressure levels (elements) with its pair or mate, with color, touch, nutrients, herbs, and homeopathic remedies—all the healing methods of the past millennia.

They are just exhibiting complex behaviors due to environmental stresses. Modern day physicians medicate their patients for these ailments, and some people just medicate themselves. However, many of these types of behaviors and predicaments were documented in medical texts of the past.

In 1926, Dr. William Boericke of Philadelphia, who had contributed to early studies in toxicology, examined the toxic effects of phosphorus poisoning. He wrote that patients with excess amounts of phosphorus in their bodies were oversensitive to external impressions, exhibited memory loss, were startled at noise, easily became excitable and fearful, were restless and fidgety, and had hot flashes.

"Today, people who work at video display terminals (VDTs) often complain of these same symptoms. Well, a lot of phosphorus is emitted from a VDT."

"Here we are inundated with phosphorus from VDTs, television, all kinds of modern gadgets."

Back in the early 1800s, Scogna said there were studies of electricity and medicine. Some theories of homeopathy are based on electric patterns of the body. Many of the elements (metals) were just then being discovered and the early homeopathists gave elements to people, observed and wrote about their reactions to these.

In the later 1800s, the factories and refineries of the Industrial Revolution began smelting those same metals and elements, creating more chemicals, and releasing toxins in the air. That activity has increased exponentially.

Scogna catalogued environmental chemicals, their effects, and their antidotes in a large volume, *The Promethion*, published in 1980.

"Today, how many people are walking around with poisons in their bodies? Do they know about these, or where they got them?"

"The knowledge from pre-industrial age homeopathy,

combined with modern technology, will bring the medicine of the future full circle", Scogna said.

"One hundred years from now, we'll redefine the word doctor", he continued. "Conventional medicine we find today is going to be something doctors of the future will almost laugh at."

"The field will be electronics, with medicines beamed by lasers, or perhaps a sonic kind of message broadcast to certain areas of the brain."

> *"There is no doubt that my patients' physical health improves exponentially faster when I add the SAF® to their treatment protocol."*
>
> —Dr. Yisroel Yaffa, MD Israel

> *"I've known that many nutritional resources work at an energy or vibrational level more than just chemically. SAF® goes beyond the chemical level. Now we have a system to focus the energy at the right level. The results are astounding, time after time."*
>
> —Dennis Clopper, Nutritionist

Infrared: New Images

It was a French woman, physicist and mathematician Emilie du Chatelet, who first postulated the infrared band in 1737.

In 1800, astronomer Sir William Herschel was trying to determine which end of the visible light spectrum emitted the most heat. He used a prism to refract white light from the sun, used a thermometer to measure the heat of the colors, and detected this band of invisible properties. He named this band Calorific Rays, after its heat properties. In 1847, it was determined by two other scientists that this type of radiation had the same properties as light, specifically that it can be reflected, refracted, and can cause interference. By the late 1800s, the term "infrared" was being used.

Infrared waves are invisible to the naked eye. It has a long wavelength, (longer than the color red, below red on the Electromagnetic (E-M) Spectrum and hence its name, "below red"). This band is found on the E-M Spectrum between visible light and radio and microwave frequencies.

What is Infrared?

Infrared radiation is energy emanating from any object having a temperature above absolute zero. Just as the light meter of a camera is able to read the amount of light given off or reflected from a subject, so special infrared detectors equipped with germanium crystals, pneumatic pressure devices, or semiconductors can measure the heat rising from objects.

Even though man had been aware of infrared for more than 200 years, it was not known what its practical application might be. As often happens, it was during a war that a use was found. In World War II, the military used infrared in heat-seeking devices to detect human bodies at night and in the fog. After the war,

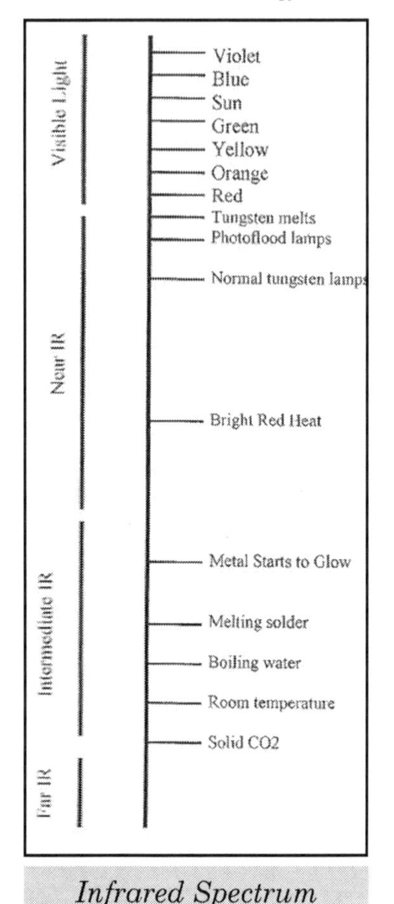

Infrared Spectrum

peaceful uses included infrared heat in homes and cooking, and in medicine, as heat, for skin and muscle conditions.

Utility companies routinely use infrared thermometers to trace energy losses from buildings. In medicine, thermal imaging is helpful to "see" inside the body. Using liquid crystal plates, different temperatures appear as brilliant color variations (colors chosen by computer), revealing areas of sensitivity (cold) and pain (heat and pressure buildup) which had been undetectable before by x-ray or sonar equipment.

Some alternative practitioners readily accepted the fact that pain could be "seen", while standard medicine still tends to address the amelioration of the physical problem of pain with drugs, analgesics and painkillers.

R. Buckminster Fuller once remarked, "In 1898, when I was three years old, electrons were discovered and didn't get into the newspapers because you couldn't see them."

In spite of all the new gadgetry and technology in our world today, 99% of reality remains invisible; it is not directly contactable by the human senses. Those in pain are asked to rate their pain level on a scale of 0-10; when the pain does not disappear, even with pain killer drugs and therapy, these patients are often viewed as hypochondriacs or in need of psychiatric evaluation.

While the controversy continued on whether or not pain could be seen, tremendous inroads were quietly being made by Joseph R. Scogna, Jr. as he catalogued stuck emotions as the cause of the specific pains and sensations.

Working in the long wavelength band of infrared (thermal emissions), Scogna found that pressure and heat were stratified pockets of energy, condensed to such a degree that they formed what is called in physics, Black Body Mass (BBM). These BBMs could be split further into positively charged (male) or negatively charged (female) BBMs.

The emotions, coined by Scogna the (e)lectric motions, or energy movements within the molecular structure of the body, lend themselves quite handily to this same analysis by infrared detectors.

Hot Emotions

The "hot" emotions or pressures, such as anger, grief, and resentment, accumulate with replays over time, until they are visible with infrared detectors as black body masses. These emotions are disruptive and create havoc in an individual's body and life. Someone who is out of harmony with his own system (on spirit, mind, and or body levels) breeds trouble for himself as his own health risks increase.

The only way to observe or detect the black body mass of hidden, unwanted energies and emotions is by utilizing the channel of the BBM itself— the brain and the mind— which seem to have brought these into being in the first place!

A very simplistic method for understanding human energy patterns is accomplished with a galvanometer or an electrical meter, in use since the mid-1800s. One merely attaches oneself to either, recalls a past traumatic experience, and watches as the meter reacts to the condensed energies drifting by. However, these apparatuses are not specific enough as to function, content, and whether or not it possesses positive or negative charge.

An acupuncturist, or one schooled in traditional Chinese or Asian medicine, understands this concept: the hot or stuck energy as blocked chi; and where it is absent or flowing too rapidly, this practitioner knows to slow it down.

Quantum Leaps

It is in this area that Joseph Scogna made quantum leaps when he catalogued these negative emotional states as to electrical charge, substance, and content.

Unlike the medical use of liquid crystals, which display fabricated colors and do not record actual temperatures, the Infrared Sensitizer used in SAF® registers specific temperatures at certain and precise locations following the meridian points or junctions of brain and mind where energy impacts and accumulates. These hot and cold readings were transposed by a converter into the mathematical matrix unique to the SAF® computing system. A specific sequence of numbers appears, which relates to the stressed organs and glands, the emotions in play, and various other designations.

A complete explanation and the numbering system of the science of SAF® is explained in detail in Scogna-authored books, such as ***SAF Simplified*** and in various training material available for students.

The precise locations of energy accumulation are centers of gravity within the body based on grids of vector geometry— these are called the Gravinometric Points. Each point represents a location where three organ and gland systems vent or release their heat. Taking temperatures at each of these sites, and interfacing the reads with the SAF® matrix creates a sequence of numbers, which can then be read in the standard way. See page 17 or back cover for face template of points to follow.

Three-Dimensional Scans

Scogna's initial use of infrared was on a flat, two-dimensional plane. He had theorized that the actual electric and magnetic nature of the symptoms, diseases and traumas of a person could be tracked. His work led to the understanding that there were definite entities involved for each specific disease or syndrome; that certain entities had affinity for particular organs and glands. The initial two-dimensional scanning gave SAF® practitioners a view of the precise symmetry of energy patterns in the body.

As Scogna related: "In those first scans, the #19 (skin), never appeared in a chain. Not once. The infrared device was using the skin as part of its scanning matrix, as its means for data entry. The reads revealed which organs/glands were heating up and which organs/glands were cooling down. We could see there was an overload in certain areas."

The flat plane scans were followed by three-dimensional scanning techniques, and this allowed the computer matrix to present the skin (#19). This three-dimensional scanning, that is, the points where three organ and gland systems vent and release their heat, are located on the following page.

For example, referring to the Gravinometric Face Points (page 17), Point #1 (Medial Supra Frontalis) is the venting site for the mind (14), the hypothalamus & the senses (15), and the endocrine system (17/18). Point #2 (Right Supra Temporalis) is the venting site for the liver (6), thyroid (10) and posterior pituitary (21). Point #18 (Left Orbicularis Oris) is the venting site for the colon (3), sex organs (8) and skin (19).

It is a complex system that took much effort to create and test, but lends itself easily to the SAF® matrix.

Infrared as used in SAF® proves the theory that

energies can know and intersect with other energies and be translated.

SAF® is no longer sold as a separate computing system for an office setting. Instead, a much-improved version is now available as a complete system, and can be accessed by subscription from all parts of the world with most modern browsers.

SAF® Online enables the practitioner and the researcher to find Interpretations for the chain, as well as Remedies based on combinations of the metabolic doubles (two numbers) in the chain.

A vast assortment of Interpretations and Remedies are available to excite and satisfy any type of practitioner, from an acupuncturist, massage therapist, energetic healer, naturopath, medical doctor, nurse practitioner, dietician, psychologist to a juice devotee and all healers in between (see Part Two, pages 55-87).

"Joseph Scogna's use of infrared to catalog the venting sites of the nervous system is a monumental leap forward in the evaluation of human physiology, psychology, and spirituality. This brilliant researcher, with a mind of the 21st century and way beyond that, has given us a dynamic new dimension, a unified approach to our holistic health status - past, present, and future.

In the years to come, the application of SAF® and Infrared technology will be one of the most wonderful blessings to mankind."

—John Abdo, ND, PhD (endocrinology, nutrition)
Dayspring International, San Antonio, TX
www.DrJohnAbdo.com

Gravinometric Face Points

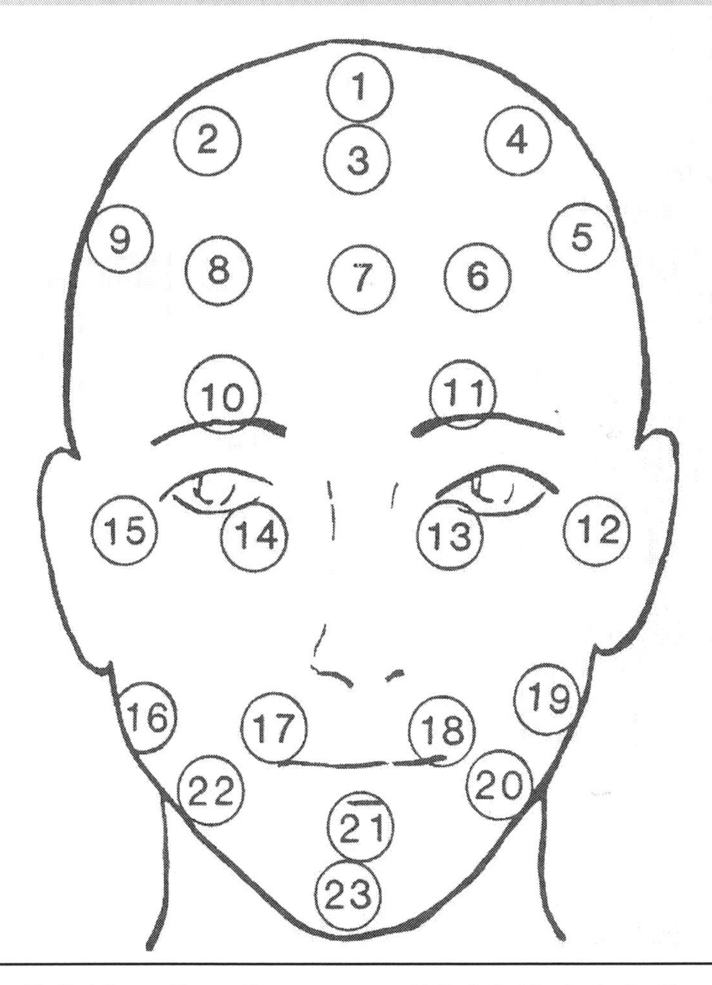

1. Medial Supra Frontalis
2. Right Supra Temporalis
3. Supra Frontalis
4. Left Supra Temporalis
5. Left Temporalis
6. Left Frontalis
7. Frontalis
8. Right Frontalis
9. Right Temporalis
10. Right Corrugator Depresser
11. Left Corrugator Depresser
12. Left Temporomandibular Joint
13. Left Orbicularis Oculi
14. Right Orbicularis Oculi
15. Right Temporomandibular Joint
16. Right Masseter
17. Right Orbicularis Oris
18. Left Orbicularis Oris
19. Left Masseter
20. Left Platysma
21. Orbicularis Oris
22. Right Platysma
23. Mentalis

Operating Infrared with SAF®

First, familiarize yourself with the infrared device and make sure all previously logged data have been deleted (see Clear the Memory, page 21). Access your SAF® Online account at LifeEnergyResearch.com.

Choose your client's file, click "Enter Infrared Data" and the infrared template for temperature values will be displayed on the screen. Have your client sit comfortably in a chain. Remove glasses and clear forehead of hair.

Log a complaint, then follow How to Take an Infrared Scan, next page.

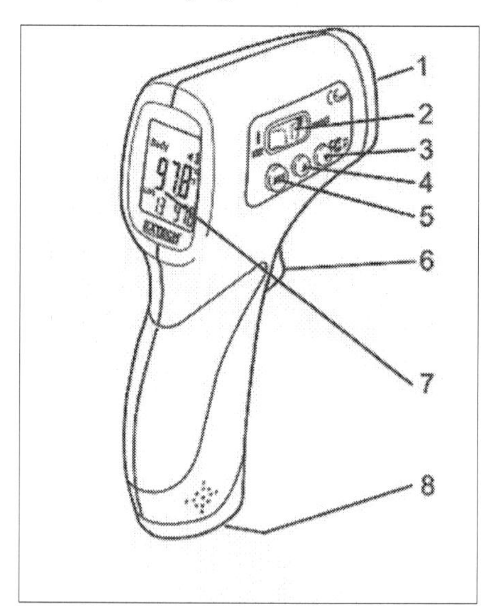

ExTech IR 200
Meter Description

1 IR sensor
2 Body-Surface switch
3 Down button
4 Up button
5 Mode button
6 Measurement trigger
7 LCD display
8 Battery compartment

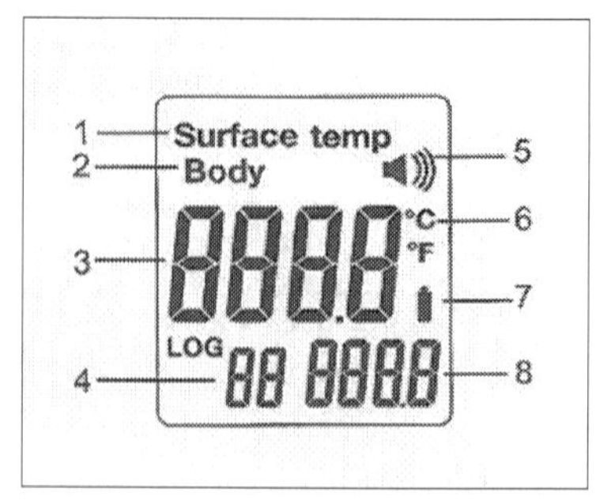

LCD Display

1 Surface mode
2 Body mode
3 Temperature display
4 Memory location (by number)
5 Alarm active (beeps)
6 Temperature units (C-F)
7 Low battery icon
8 Memory temperature display

Operating Instructions for the ExTech IR200

The IR 200 device is recommended for all SAF® scanning. There is no laser light for sighting; safety of the eyes is a consideration when scanning the face.

Surface Temperature Mode Settings

The Surface temperature is the mode to use with SAF® scanning. We have found in clinical work that facial hair and animal fur will not distort the read when in Surface mode.

With the meter off, press the MODE button once to set the C/F temperature units (Celsius/Fahrenheit). The temperature units will flash. Press the UP or DOWN button to change the unit.

Fahrenheit (F) works best as it offers a wider range in degrees. If the operator of this device lives in a country that follows Celsius, or has customarily used the Celsius scale, please note, for the purpose of SAF® infrared technology, the actual temperature per Gravinometric Point is not as important as the variation of degrees between points. We are looking for the hot points and the cool points and this will vary person to person. So please use the (F) reading for Fahrenheit.

How to Take an Infrared Scan for SAF®

1. Set the body-surface switch for **Surface** for wide range surface measurements.
2. Hold the meter by its handle and point it toward the surface to be measured.
3. Follow the Gravinometric Face Point Chart. Hold the infrared device 1-2 inches from Point #1.
4. Press the trigger to turn the meter on and take the first temperature reading. A “beep” is heard as this occurs. The temperature reading appears in the large display and the logged data number

and value appear in the smaller display.

5. Temperature numbers can be typed immediately into the template provided on the computer screen, or stored in memory in the device for entering later on.
6. Release the trigger and the reading will hold for approximately 7 seconds after which the meter will automatically shut off, saving the read in memory. Trigger presses can occur up to a rate of one per second to quickly log samples.
7. Continue to take temperature readings in sequence at each of the 23 points. Either enter into the template immediately or store in logged memory, as stated in 5 above.
8. If the temperature reading is greater than 140F or 60C, HI will appear in the display. For our purposes, this is an incorrect read and should be redone.
9. If the temperature dips below 32F or 0C, LO will appear in the display. For our purposes, this is an incorrect read and should be redone.
10. Once scan is complete (make sure a complaint is logged), hit submit and the chain and data is filed and at the same time appears on the computer screen, ready to be deciphered.

Data Memory – Retrieving the Temperatures

For use when saving the temperature readings in memory.

To review the logged data values, while the unit is OFF, press both the UP and DOWN buttons until the memory log and its temperature are displayed. Use the UP or DOWN buttons to scroll through the memory locations. Starting with #1, log the temperature into the infrared template on the computer screen, position #1. The device will shut off after about 7 seconds.

If this is not enough time for transferring to the

computer template, either write the temperatures down to log later, or have someone else read the temperature values as you type them in.

In the future, consider logging these values in as they are taken (see #5, above).

Clear the Memory

To clear logged data, press both UP and DOWN buttons, then scroll through to the 0 memory location an press the MODE button. The unit will beep twice to indicate memory has been cleared.

Battery Replacement

When the low battery symbol appears on the display, replace the meter's batteries. The battery compartment is located on the bottom of the handle. Open the compartment by removing one screw and sliding the cover off. Replace the 2 AA batteries and close the battery compartment.

IR Measurement Notes

- Before measuring, be sure to clean surfaces that are covered with frost, oil, grime, etc.
- The Extech IR200 meter automatically compensates for deviations in ambient room temperature. However, it can take up to 30 minutes for the meter to adjust to extremely wide changes.
- The Extech IR200 meter should be recalibrated on a yearly basis. The manufacturer, named in the booklet that came with the boxed unit, completes this service.

The Infrared and its Scientific Applications

Excerpt from Project Isis: The Fundamentals of Human Electricity, as printed in the Life Energy Monitor.

A meter is a necessary apparatus to use in any type of investigative work or research analysis, in order to understand the effects of mind, body, and spirit. When we are trying to observe human electricity or any other type of phenomenon connected with the activity of electron movement in the body, we must immediately elicit help with the standard scanning of some type of electrical measuring instrument. It is extremely important that we use a standard instrument, so that our own particular bias does not influence our learning process. It is mandatory for scientific research to have such devices.

In studying the human body, we must utilize instruments that can measure the transference of electrons, which will be indicative of the cause-effect relationship of power, concept, energy, and mass in the system. To state it simply, the research scientist studying the human body and the human framework of electric circuits would be lost without a meter.

The infrared sensitizer (sometimes called The Gun with its particular use by Joe Scogna and Life Energy Research) is a necessary implement for the study of the transference of heat, electromagnetic wave phenomena and electrons themselves. Without this device, in coordination with specific SAF® computer programs and databases (now available at SAF Online), many of the research projects could not have been carried out.

Much of the emission of radiation coming from the body will automatically respond to data that correlates to the mass, energy and concept formulas, which create power. If a person has a particular disease condition, it is often extremely easy to track this condition by the use of infrared devices in conjunction with Interpretation modules. The sophistication of testing programs that have been developed for the infrared surpasses any other type of metering devices that have been developed to this date.

The galvanometric skin response, or conductance and resistance meters, used to measure relay and switch points on the human body, are subject to the frailties of contact that is necessary in that type of analysis. This is also the case with bio-feedback, frequency generators and other such devices in use today.

Any disease process has its own specific voltage ranges, and if we were to induct a current into a section of the body that was sick, the electrical configuration of the electrons, protons and atoms would change. (Electric stimulation used for physical therapy relies on this fact to achieve results).

By using **noninvasive, non-contact infrared sensing** equipment, the body can remain in its specific state while being monitored very cleanly and efficiently. In other words, by not touching the body, the sensor does not disturb the delicate electron patterns that are being transmitted by a disease condition or memory of a traumatic event.

For analyzation purposes, we need to be able to stand back and take a "photograph" of the individual by using a noninvasive sensor. For this reason it is highly recommended that all sensing devices in the future be of this noninvasive type.

The infrared sensor is tracking the electric potential that has built up in a certain gland, organ or even cell or tissue, as a result of the individual's experiences in the environment of his life.

In most high-speed infrared sensing equipment, the

> *"In the final analysis, the metering of an individual with infrared devices will be the only method to use in the future."*
>
> —Joseph R. Scogna, Jr.

particular tracking device that is used (high-speed vidicon TV camera) is much too rapid to pick up specific potentials that relate to primary disease patterns. Not only are these extremely expensive, they are too fast. For our purposes, simple infrared spot detectors are much more efficacious.

The spot detector (Extech IR200), which will measure one (1) centimeter in diameter to an accuracy of one-tenth (.10) degree, +/-2%, will be able to scan specific areas of voltage potential and electron movement. By observing these two particular phenomena in the system, the practitioner or researcher is able to actually track the experience of the human body. This means that all pain, sensation, injury or upset, which may precipitate into chronic emotion, attitude and concept anomalies, can be observed.

This type of sophisticated scanning process is necessary for the evaluation of modern man. We must catch up with the science and the integrity of instrumentation on the planet today, so that we can equalize our battle against poisons, pollution and toxins that are being proliferated in the environment.

All manner of electron transfer can be observed with the correct metering procedures. The exact temperature, which is recorded on most infrared sensing devices, is a specific readout of black body radiation and black body masses in the system. In actuality, the sensor is measuring voltage changes, current and amplitude. The amplification of poison in the system automatically shows imbalances of primary energy formulas necessary to maintain a wholesome human structure.

The movement of energy around the body also has

the capability to "vent" through certain reflex areas, which are designated sites for organ relief. The schematic or wiring diagram for the body is impressive. Intense research projects have been launched to map out the entire electronic network and passageways of information from organ and gland systems and areas to the periphery of the body. Evidently, the brain and nervous system, in coordination with the endocrine system, the energy system and the circulatory system, has a sympathetic order that allows reflex points to vent electrons whenever positive pressure begins to build up in any part of the body.

These venting sites are places on the body that can be noted with infrared sensing devices. At the venting sites, black body radiation is emitted as a response to the buildup of black body masses in the brain, the nervous system and the endocrine organs. The SAF® practitioner, armed with an infrared sensor and the various Interpretations, is able to observe the direct relationship of toxins, poisons, vermin, bacteria and any other entity that has enough voltage potential to interfere with, or jam circuitry in the body.

Specific reflex points on the face, hands, feet, and other vital areas of the body (such as the spine) have venting sites which, when measured in particular patterns or "rhythms", can give an idea of the sequences of black body mass and black body radiation in the brain, nervous system and the endocrine system, which create particular masses or realities of diseases and disorders. Apparently, what scientists and medical researchers were cataloging as disease entities for years, were merely the reflections of the interaction of voltage changes and electron transfer in the system, in response to black body mass and black body radiation pressures in the brain, the nervous system and the endocrine system.

The particular image of disease (such as acne,

The Axioms of SAF®

1. Each of the 24 organ systems (thymus, heart, colon, stomach, liver, pancreas, etc.) has a life of its own. All are connected to the nervous system.

2. The organ systems sometimes work alone, but many times work in unison with other systems.

3. Various amounts of energy are assigned to the organ systems by the brain/mind complex on a specific time table.

4. Any extreme stress or trauma such as accidents, drugs, operations, etc., freeze or lock up a pattern of energy into a non-operational status at the exact instant of impact.

5. Non-operational status of organ systems can be plotted by the special 64 point patented secret mathematical matrix and flow diagram generated by infrared detection.

6. Once detected, the <u>non-operational status</u> can be deprogrammed to a new state of free operation, thereby releasing all injury - past, present and future.

"What Joe Scogna so capably gets across is that instead of throwing up our hands in surrender, there is beauty and balance that went into the creation of this process called life." —Mark Stern, M.D.

herpes, congenital anomalies, diabetes, heart disease, cancer, etc.) is a final effect of a long-term electrical power relationship between environmental hazards and hindrances, and internal confusion or inability to cope with specific disharmonies or harmonies of the environment. When we observe a disease condition, we are viewing a reflex pattern of electron transfer and voltage changes, which can be rectified by the correct application of proper supplemental materials such as vitamins, minerals, enzymes, laser treatment, water, flower essences, foods, physical activity, sound, color, pressure, emotional release work, etc.; literally thousands of therapeutics can be used. However, these materials and modalities must be tracked and understood fully to gain awareness about their habits, moods and methodologies. (See the complex list of the SAF® Online Interpretations and Remedies)

The instrument that is used for infrared scanning of the body can direct and coordinate many of the operations of supplementation by specific materials and nutrients, which can change the electron flow, or the voltage in the body.

The voltage potential and the power of the body are synonymous. Someone who is in the throes of a disease condition has evidently been interfered with by some outside energy that is effectively blocking transmissions from one end of the body to the other. Without some type of specific testing device, such as the infrared spot detector, the ability of the practitioner to track the disease condition from moment to moment is greatly diminished. This is true because the infrared device can actually monitor the electron transfer from moment to moment, to specifically designate whether or not the voltage potential and power of the disease process is being attenuated or aggravated.

The change of the condition is an extremely important monitoring procedure, which is necessary to alert the practitioner when to start the program, or application of modalities, and more importantly, when to stop the application. Many times, clients and participants who have been corrected and adjusted, find themselves being continually dosed with some material or some treatment they no longer need. The infrared sensor is precise and accurate enough to alert the physician or practitioner that the process is over when a specific type of voltage potential presents itself (infrared sensing voltage potentials are measured as a directly proportional reality to temperature). The practitioner can observe this potential as an unnecessary part of the individual's organism.

For example, if we were to observe a wart on someone's face, we could also view around the wart the exact genetic detail lines that were dictated by the DNA and RNA blueprint. The wart is an excrescence that is unnecessary to the function of the face; it is a symbol of some disharmonic value or a disharmonic metabolic operation somewhere in the body. We can easily experience these phenomena visually. A wart is disturbing to the sight sense but, because the visible light spectrum is only 1/80th of the entire electromagnetic spectrum, it is probable that most of the disease conditions reside in invisible areas of the electromagnetic spectrum. Conversely, an individual's face may look pleasant enough, but in actuality may suffer from warts, tumors and other unsightly manifestations of energy on invisible wavelengths and frequencies.

This is a reality; this is science, and is something that can be measured.

Infrared devices can observe energies in areas of the body on electromagnetic wavelengths that are unseen, unfelt and even unknown. In effect, it can scan and find specific activity that is counter-opposed to the normal operation of the body in areas of the body's electromagnetic spectrum, which are invisible to the naked eye. Once able to observe these invisibilities, the practitioner can cope with something plaguing the individual, causing him distress, discomfort, pain, sensation and more probably, bizarre, unwanted emotions, attitudes and erroneous thought processes that are detrimental to his or her survival.

Using the Interpretations and Remedies at SAF Online will present a means for change.

In the final analysis, the metering of clients with infrared devices will be the only method to use in the future. The changing of the human condition from disharmonic to harmonic necessitates the ability on the part of the practitioner or the individual himself to be able to sense or scan the exact condition of the body, not merely in degrees of temperature or by sense perception, but right down to the bare electrons.

(right) The ExTech IR200, a simple handheld unit, is the infrared of choice for SAF® practitioners.
Purchase separately through Amazon.
Temperature values can be entered immediately into the Infrared template in your SAFonline account or stored in memory in the unit until you access the Internet later.

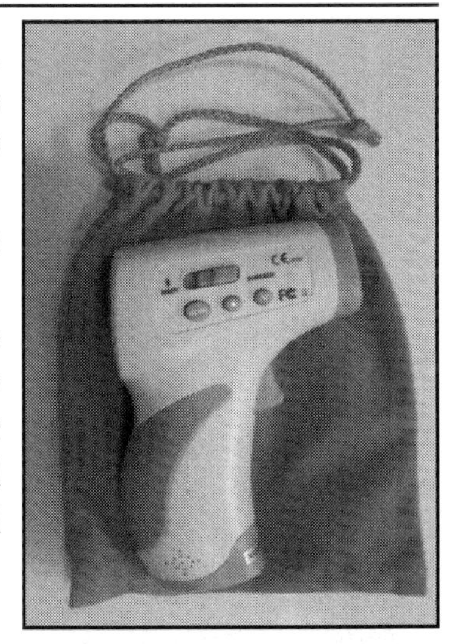

It is a breeze for anyone to learn; faster chain creation than the questionnaires. Excellent for scanning the infirm, children and even pets!

Researcher claims Infrared Sensor Gun can find Symptom Patterns

by William Bradley, Reading Eagle Staff Writer

An articulate young man brandishing an odd-looking gun confronted more than 20 persons in the UGI Corp's Flame Room Monday night.

The gunslinger identified himself as Joseph R. Scogna, Jr., founder and director of the Life Energy Research Foundation, Inc. Mt Penn, Pennsylvania.

But Scogna told them he wanted to lift up the audience, not hold them up.

The gun, which senses the body's circulatory patterns, is being tested as a medical diagnostic tool and is being used by 24 doctors across the country.

In a meeting sponsored by the Berks County Natural Living Club, Scogna explained that the infrared hand-held sensor gun has almost unlimited applications.

"EVERYPLACE I go, people have an awful lot of bewilderment about what I'm teaching," Scogna said. "But aren't we getting a little tired of being poked at, shot at and radiated?"

"It's really very, very simple," he continued as he squeezed the trigger. "Areas of the body that have a lack of blood are cold and areas of the body that are hot have a surge of blood."

Scogna explained that infrared means the energy is below and beyond the red spectrum of light.

"The visible light spectrum contains things you can see, feel and touch," he explained.

"But there's also a body of energy "infra", or beyond, what you can see and it's not voodoo or mumbo jumbo," he stressed. "That body of energy details the body's balance and can be tapped by using infrared sensing."

left: Joseph R. Scogna demonstrates how the infrared sensor he developed can help a doctor find a patient's patterns and syndromes without sticking him with needles or bombarding him with radiation.

Photo by J. Sheridan Evans

Scogna has refined the process of thermography —a photographic technique which measures and records infrared heat patterns—down to the hand-held sensor that gives an exact pattern of heat radiation with precise temperature values.

He explained that the data can be fed into a computer enabling a good practitioner to quickly pinpoint a patient's symptom patterns or syndromes.

"THIS DEVICE is so confident that you have enough radiation bouncing off your body that it isn't even equipped with a flashbulb," he said as the audience burst into laughter.

Pulling out the hand-held sensor, the Philadelphia native said the device gives a moment-by-moment diagram of an individual's energy patterns, which is expressed in numerical values on the heel of the unit.

"This thing," he said, "sort of hunts down the spooks."

A researcher and author of more than 50 books on nutrition, physics, symptom patterns, homeopathy and related fields, Scogna said the device can pinpoint a patient's syndromes without invading the body with needles or bombarding it with radiation.

"It doesn't take the place of a doctor," he emphasized. "The doctor really has to stay right on top of this latest research in energetics and take advantage of this technology. We've been able to create and use this infrared sensor along with our computing system at a far more affordable price and with greater efficacy than standard hospital units."

The host of the "Help Yourself To Health" television show on Berks Community Television, Scogna noted that infrared sensing had its first practical applications during World War II.

"THEY USED infrared to "heat seek" and find hot objects such as people in tanks in the woods," he explained. "It would just look through the darkness, find people and then they would do nasty things to them."

As the technique became more sophisticated, Scogna said that snipers not only could see the targets, but could also look inside the bodies of the targets.

"It's kind of strange that what was primarily used in the military is now being used today to detect breast cancer," Scogna said. "We use it to find the psychosomatic or energetic hot spots. For our purposes, we are tracking the emotions involved, those that are creating heat, pressure and troubles for a person. Our computing unit will help doctors treat each patient as a unique individual, which they are, based on the symptom and syndrome patterns presented."

"SAF® is not medical diagnosis. All physical diseases have underlying emotional causes—some may be very deep indeed—so it is this aspect of the human being that we address in the science of SAF®" —Joseph R. Scogna, Jr.

Thermography and Your Emotions

Originally published in the Life Energy Monitor.

An incredible event has occurred.

Throughout history, man has been inspired to put simple inventions to multifarious human use. This has again been accomplished. There is a new union and partnership between man and machine.

Such discoveries as electricity and the internal combustion engine have been put to work in so many various ways for mankind that these wonders, which started out as a simple spark and chug, are now literally the most ubiquitous servo-mechanisms on the planet.

The latest marvel is the discovery of infrared sensing. Joseph R Scogna, Jr has bridged the gap between man's emotional response mechanisms and infrared technology. By cataloging infrared images and temperatures of the effect of negative emotions (anger, resentment, hostility, grief, sorrow, and hatred, etc) he has been able to provide a reliable system for detecting deep-set emotional disturbance patterns.

The thermogram is the term used for an image made with an infrared sensing device, which records the heat escaping from the body. Since the neuro-vascular system, that is, the network of nerves assisting the flow of blood via the circulatory system (veins, arteries, vessels, etc), can be tapped or monitored by infrared "heat-seeking" devices, incredible silhouettes of life energy in its forming stages can be manufactured. These pictures present a diagram of energy or a blueprint to follow when mapping the cause and effect of negative emotional states.

The astounding thing, however, is the ease with which Scogna's SAF® sensitizer detects bottled up emotions. Apparently, infrared layers itself over time and by adding the correct mathematical matrix to an already brilliant system, Scogna has been able to "trace" in time the exact moments when severe emotional upsets have occurred. This process has been done on thousands with the same relentless accuracy; and I was one of them.

With utmost ease, the sensitizer detected an upset that had occurred in my life. Thirty-two years ago!

I had mentioned to Scogna while I was in this interview that my stomach ached, and he had casually said, "Let's talk to it."

I wasn't used to talking to my stomach. He explained that infrared radiation is produced by the genes themselves. In a human body, the DNA instructs the RNA to perform actions for the genetic plan. This action requires the use of amino acids, which in turn control many enzymatic catalysts in the system. The resultant movement of energy and transfer of power produces a perfunctory load of HEAT; not just plain heat, but heat in a specific pattern. He claimed his sensitizer unit could trace 10^{24} patterns on 880 channels, in 128 variant signals, sensing signals. That's an astronomical number. I asked him how he could remember all these patterns and he said with a deadpan look, "It's a tough job, but somebody has to do it."

I already knew that he had conducted fifteen years of research into life energy, had written more than 200 texts, papers, pamphlets, books, 300 computer programs, and 50 separate main databases; all he had to do was access them to get to the data he wanted.

But I wanted to know why my stomach hurt. The process was simple and efficient. It didn't take more than five minutes.

As I exposed my tummy flesh he merely trained the sensitizer unit at my sore spot and then, cued by the sound of beep noises coming from the computer, he moved the gun-like apparatus from spot to spot until he had made a criss-cross web, called a matrix, one inch from my abdomen.

After several moments, a mathematical string was

produced, a numerical sentence, an SAF® chain of integers. Then the magic seemed to occur. The numbers that represented my stomach picture had a "story" about my stomach in them.

I asked Scogna to interpret these numbers but he begged off. "This isn't voodoo or psychic phenomena, you know," he said in his sedate style. "This is about you. You're going to decipher it yourself."

And I did. He had reference books of enormous sizes. He directed me to discover and learn the causes of my stomach upset. He warned me first that all physical upsets are preceded by emotional ones, and it didn't matter how long ago the emotional upset had occurred.

My number chain was: 23-7-3-1-12-14-24-5-15-20-21. These numbers represented pressure gradations of heat radiation emanating from my stomach and the symbols held the stuck or frozen picture of the emotional upset within their cryptic messages.

One reference book said the upset was thirty-two years ago. I was only 3 years old then and I couldn't remember the events of my life very well when I was that age. Nothing came to mind. I insisted there were no emotional upsets that could possibly cause my (as I now confessed) rather chronic stomach trouble of today.

But Scogna urged me to be patient and allow the mental review to awaken the emotion story buried deep inside my mind.

Researching further in the tomes, the chain now gave emotional "clues" as to what the trauma could have been. The number 14 (the core) suggested the overall emotional trouble. When I looked this up, it said, "worry". That was true, I did worry. But I have always considered my "worrying" to be a conscientious enthusiasm for my work.

Scogna asked: "Can worry affect your stomach?"

Yes, of course, I reasoned. The more I thought, the angrier my stomach became. But this didn't prove anything. I couldn't change being a worrier anyway, because I didn't know what made me worry in the first place. I guess I was just born that way.

Scogna then had me look up #23, the lead or first number in my chain. It said "rejection."

My hair stood on end. My boyfriend and I had just separated two months before and I was worried about him. In fact, I couldn't get him out of my mind. On top of that, I had lost twelve pounds, which would have been terrific for some people, but I only weighed 110 to begin with. I was now less than 100 pounds; the thing with my boyfriend was making me anorectic.

I looked at Scogna and he was expressionless; as if he knew I would find this out. But my real problem wasn't solved. Why was I behaving so irrationally about my split up with Sam? I wanted to do it. It was my idea. I guessed it was just sympathy, but I was mentally, emotionally and also physically confused.

Scogna said in a routine manner, "Do you have an idea of the emotional trauma that occurred thirty-two years ago?"

I almost saw red. He was acting like the trauma was really there, yet I couldn't see it. I was stirred up and ready to cry for some reason and he persisted in wanting to know about some obscure event in the deep recesses of my mind, where I had no recollection.

My eyes welled up with tears, but he ignored my transient emotional condition and pointed to what he called the anchor number at the right end of the chain, and there sat "21". The reference book explained: "Grief over a loss."

Scogna asked quietly, "Thirty-two years ago, who did you lose?"

The picture of her face seemed to explode into my mental screen. My mother! It hit me hard. Her smiling face, smooth and shining with youth, framed by soft dark curls, no hint of grey. She left me at the nursery school! The first day. I had cried and cried; I couldn't stop. I went on a hunger strike and refused to eat at

SAF® Operative Chart

(Endocrine Sense Channels)

	Condition LEAD	Organ CORE	Mid-Emotion ANCHOR
1.	protection	thymus	aggression
2.	synchronize	heart	love
3.	detoxify	colon	hate
4.	digestion	stomach	happy
5.	coordinate	anterior pituitary	observant
6.	transmutation	liver	sadness
7.	vaporization	lungs	monotony
8.	reproduction	sex organs	apathy
9.	locomotion	bones/muscles	pain
10.	metabolization	thyroid	anxiety
11.	circulation	veins/arteries	resentment
12.	electrification	brain	nervousness
13.	capacitance	adrenals	courage
14.	analyzation	mind	wonder
15.	evaluation	senses	attention
16.	filtration	kidneys	fear
17/18.	equalize	endocrine	conservative
19.	demarcation	skin	boredom
20.	location	pancreas	laughter
21.	liquification	posterior pituitary	grief
22.	experience	parathyroid	anger
23.	rejection	spleen	antagonize
24.	acceptance	lymph	enthusiasm

The above chart with mid-emotions is the language of SAF®, how we are able to read the messages (symptoms) our body is sending us via the chain sequence.

The complete Endocrine Sense Channels Chart is presented in Junk DNA: Unlocking the Hidden Secrets of Your DNA. It includes the triple emotions - mid-emotions, low emotions (shadow side) and high emotions (spiritual side), reflecting the dichotomy of vibrational elements and balance (vice and virtue) as often used in Eastern healing modalities (TCM and TAM).

Mom

snack time and my little tummy ached so bad. I had translated that loss of my mother, that emotional emptiness, into physical emptiness, hunger. I wouldn't eat.

I realized that Sam and I didn't stand a chance. We had been dating two years, but my mother had died several months ago and I mentally, emotionally, and unconsciously went on strike when she passed away. It was after that event that I refused to be with Sam. I denied myself the only person I felt good with to get back at my mother... for leaving me, first at the school, then in life. Loss.

I was suddenly unraveled and de-confused, my hunger pains made sense, and now I honestly wanted to eat something for the first time in two months.

And this was just a demonstration!

On a lark, Scogna's infrared sensitizer had changed my life and I was grateful.

Note to the Reader regarding Report at right:

In this case, Mr. Scogna ran the Infrared as a Patch program and the Interpretation was completed with SAF® texts.

Although with a complaint of "tummy ache, can't eat", one might assume the #4 (stomach) would be in the number sequence, but this is not the case.

The numbers represent the stressed organs and glands and these are trying to tell the chain-owner important information. The lead, core, and anchor tell the story, which she pieced together with the "reminder words" of SAF® texts and charts. She had emotional clues to follow.

The chain is about worry (14), which resulted in rejection in the present time (23), and is held in place by grief, loss in the past. (21).

Name: Female Writer
Age: 35
Questionnaire: Infrared
Complaint: tummy ache, can't eat

Chain: 23-7-3-1-12-14-24-5-15-20-21

Lead: 23
Core: 14
Anchor: 21

SAMPLE REPORT
Infrared Study

Operative Words with Ages
Stress Up-Links
Emotion Hazards
Problems Worries Upsets
Modality Sorter

Operative Words with Ages (modified to fit this space)

Age	#	Organ/Gland	Condition	Emotion
32-present	23	spleen	rejection	antagonize
16-19.2	14	mind	analyze	wonder/ worry
birth-3.2	21	post. pituitary	hydrolyze	grief

Stress Up-Links
5-15: hearing, can't distinguish words or sounds, forgets events, imagination runs wild
15-20: doctor's squint, pressure buildup in the mind and sense mechanisms

Emotion Hazards
————————self-abnegation (acute)

Problems Worries Upsets
————————Being worried
————————Being right

Modality Sorter
————————Religion/Philosophy
————— Get withhold out
—— Misunderstood Situation Correction
————— Acupressure
————————Writing

By using the Infrared to create a sequence and accessing SAF Online (www.LifeEnergyResearch.com), the Generate Report feature presented this case above (modified to fit). Much more information can be uncovered for this sequence of numbers, all available at the speed of a keystroke!

"Just like Tesla, some spirits arrive well before their time—it's a great challenge to be a forerunner. Joseph Scogna pulled back the veil of time to show us a new understanding of ourselves and instill the courage to act and embrace what is needed, and how to heal in these challenging times.....Thanks for keeping the treasure of his knowledge alive and available!"

—Bruce L. Erickson
Santa Barbara, CA

Project Isis: The Fundamentals of Human Electricity (8" x 10"; 234 pages; $21.95)

www.KathyScogna.com

Life Energy and Human Electricity!

Joe Scogna describes human electricity in electrical terms (voltage, current, ohms) as this best illustrates the transference of energy and communication among the body systems, and between the body (mass), mind (energy) and spirit (concept).

You'll learn how we create POWER and ENERGY, how our mental images are formed and stored, and about the effects of mass-energy imbalance, when someone might ask of us:"What's the matter?"

Human Electric Current

Excerpt from Project Isis: The Fundamentals of Human Electricity.

Current is the term used for the movement of particles and electrons against the movement of other electrons or particles, which cause a resistance to the flow. Considering the image of a person trying to run a mile in less than four minutes, we can see that the human body is beset by many specific kinds of resistances in the environment. If we intend the human body to move at a certain rate, we'll be automatically confronted with the environmental hindrances that are themselves resistances that we all face every day.

Environmental Energy Inhibits Our Own Energy

The flow, or current, of energy in the environment directly inhibits the flow of our own current of energy. If the environment were much less inhibiting with much less current, such as on the surface of the moon, we would be able to run a mile in less than a minute. Depending on the amount of resistance in the environment, we can do just about anything we wish. However, as in most cases, all activities are governed by a specific amount of resistance, and we can measure the amount of current that is needed by the human body to perform a certain function.

One way of looking at the idea of energy measurement is through the activity of lifting weights. If we were to lift a 50-pound barbell, we would need a certain amount of electrical transmittance; the exchange of energy forces from the nervous system to the muscles, in order to move the weights up and down. The amount of current that is available is directly proportionate to the integrity of the system. If our own mechanism (body, mind, spirit) is beset by crosscurrent and interference, then we will be much weaker than someone who has spent a lifetime clearing out the blockages and barriers or energies that inhibit his control. If we were to pick up the 50-pound weight and curl it toward our chest, we would immediately be able to gauge just how much current we possessed; if we could get it up one time and release it, then we would have a certain measurable amount of current. (In weight lifting this is called one repetition.) If we could lift the weights to our chest again, then we would have two repetitions. When we exercise, we break down the resistance or barriers between the mind's desire, the nervous system, and the muscles that do the work, so that so much weight can be displaced over a certain distance. It is the movement of weight multiplied by the number of times the action is done, which gives us a measurement of just how much current is being used.

Current Flow in the Body

The willingness of the system to carry electron flow from one location of the body to another is measured as actual current flow. The productivity of an individual is the measurement. The amount of work that we accomplish is the level of current that we possess, because current is merely a measure of work done. We could wake up in the morning and begin to assess all of the activities that we can complete, such as brushing our teeth, eating breakfast, etc.; this could be construed as the actual tally of current to be used in the system. If we wanted, we could set up an electric meter to measure the flow of electrons that would occur throughout the body for these specific actions.

One of the premier methods of determining the body's productivity is the measurement of the burning of calories. This caloric expression can be easily measured with the aid of infrared devices. (In 1800, Herschel identified what he called Calorific Rays because of this band's heat properties. These rays were later called infrared).

Because infrared devices are set up to measure the exact spectrum of energy, which is the usage of heat and heat transfer, then infrared devices would be most precise for any measurement of human productivity, even on micro-levels. It is the infinitesimal level of electron exchange that baffles science today. No one could know for sure at this point just how many electrons are transferred across space in the human body during the course of the day. We could only guess, or extrapolate from information that is received, by observing the individual's productive routing.

For example, we must be able to calculate with high accuracy the amount of weight displacement of the body moving from one area of the house to the car to the office, etc. We would have to calculate every movement of muscle at every moment of the day to get the exact amount of electron transference. It is almost incomprehensible.

Movement of Energy in a Disease Process

However, when trying to locate the specific movement of energy in the body for a certain condition or disease process, the use of infrared technology would be beyond comparison, for it is the infrared detector that is able to accurately assess the amount of heat transference that is taking place, correlating this factor with electron exchange to the most minute detail (we must have a very sensitive infrared device for these purposes).

Destination of Energy

Current itself is a measurable quantity that establishes the direction, location and destination of energy messages in the body. Without the exchange of current from one area of the body to the other, the organ systems and the body structures would not know that the other parts of the body existed. They would be alone and helpless.

For example, while sitting and reading this book, we know there are people on the other side of the country or the other side of the world. All we would need to do to verify this fact would be to pick up a telephone and call someone, watch a broadcast on TV, or listen to a radio program. Other than these actions of verification, we must trust another's word that he or she has seen people on the other side of the world. In short, we need some method of dissemination or communication to keep in touch with the reality of the existence in which we live. The movement of particles or current is the only method that is available to humankind to establish contact with the outside world and within the internal structures of his own body.

Pressure

Current establishes presence or pressure. It has the capability of performing changes of energy or changes of view so that an individual can experience new vistas of existence and survival. Without the transference of electric particles, we would be doomed to a life of being frozen in place. Perhaps the first electron to cross space was the necessary effort on the part of some Intelligence to break the monotony of silence and darkness. What we see in the environment is a spray of electron particles moving very rapidly, just to create the exhilaration of existence.

Magnetic Attraction

The flow or movement of electric particles (current) has an attractive force. As it moves, it picks up speed. Energies in the body, once released, gain power on their own. They create magnetic fields. It is interesting to watch someone who is stuck in a car at a traffic light observe a jogger passing by. The driver seems to be frozen, observing with wonder an individual moving his body through space. It is a phenomenon of magnetic attraction. All electrical currents create this very same magnetic attraction. All we need to do to prove this is so is to grab a live wire. It will immediately cause the inquisitive soul to clench his fists, as if to be hanging on for dear life. (But don't try this experiment!)

When a message of energy is sent from one place to another, it bears with it the magnetic energy of knowing. And it is the same message-sending furor that has been monopolized by newspaper, television and commercial industries to attract an individual's attention to "know what is going on."

Energy Movement holds Human Together

The movement of energies in the body (its patterns of current) acts as a glue to hold the human being together. If it were not for this electron movement, the system would collapse into a pile of lifeless dust. It has been experienced by student chiropractors that they cannot get the characteristic cracking sound from adjusting the cervical vertebrae on a cadaver. Once the body is dead, it is devoid of that dynamic life force that sparked its every movement.

The excitation of energy production in the system is a result of the dreams, wishes, desires and the coordinated effort of all systems to survive in any environment and condition.

Electric Movement of Pressure marks Time

Finally, current flow marks time. Current is a precision entity that coordinates, synchronizes and chronologically establishes a field of activity in the body. The electric movement of pressure in the system, no matter how minute or great, is on a timetable. It is this clockwork pattern that in a practical way causes a joint , is on a timetable. It is this clockwork pattern that in a practical way causes a joint effort of the entire system to create power.

"Mind and Spirit energy produces a magnetic and electric attraction for toxins and traumas. This is a behavioral pattern that acts like an antenna and pulls these in to the body.

The content of the trauma is a powerful mechanism affectionately labeled "The Dragon" in SAF® Whatever a person visualizes as his dragon, has certainly become his dragon."

(excerpts from ***SAF Simplified)***

"The Best Way Out is Always Through....."

Robert Frost, "A Servant to Servants" 1914

For Spiritual Seekers:

Although it may seem we thinking, sentient beings should be able to access the divine in us as our birthright, this is not always the case. Why not?

The shadow side stands in our way. This area is unconscious to us, and holds the most painful events and aspects of ourselves. It also exerts tremendous influence, unbeknownst to us until we bring it into the light of consciousness.

We cannot ignore or by-pass our shadow side; we must confront our dragons, as we say in SAF® parlance.

An SAF® Infrared scan will find those unconscious areas rapidly and easily. With SAF® chain work, the formerly unknown can become known again. Once remembered, the visuals will be there for us, minus the negatively -charged, condensive energy these held suspended in time.

In the SAF® process, energy is released for our use. We become more free as spiritual beings.

Yes, for all of us, the best way out is always through.

A Winning Hand - 4 ACES and a Wild Card

1. Trace it. The chain of numbers tells of the emotions & ages.
2. Face it. Acknowledge the trauma and the code.
3. Embrace it. I'm grateful for the trauma; it taught me something.
4. Replace it. It worked then but not now. Time for new codes!
5. Erase it. Delete old codes; they no longer influence me.

This WILD CARD wins the hand!

Jim Manegold, SAF Practitioner

Joe Scogna, SAF® and the Horse

Foreword Note: Joe Scogna had developed and written a unique system called the Self Awareness Formulas (SAF®), which included holistic health evaluations and questionnaires, books, and training courses for practitioners. Amazingly enough, the Life Energy System was computerized in the early 1980s when very few people were even aware of computer use.

Scogna's greatest achievement was his cutting-edge use of infrared to read the bio-energetic field and locate the nervous system venting sites. These infrared temperatures were fed into his computing system, run through various sorters and programs to reveal some incredible connections and achieve enlightening outcomes on body, mind and spirit levels. The SAF® computing system was large and heavy as early computers were, but the results were so fantastic it seemed to be from an episode of the TV version of Star Trek! Indeed, Joe had always longed for a Tri-Corder, the handheld diagnosing device of Dr. McCoy, but that is another story.....

Roger Willoughby-Ray, of Pittsburgh, Penna, recounted a funny experience with Joe Scogna and SAF®. Roger was a well-known communications expert (President of Willoughby Communications) and marketing consultant for Francis Health Systems throughout the USA, plus an import/export specialist.

A well-known radio personality, Roger spoke with a delightful English accent. Being an advocate of computers and self-improvement, he was enthralled with the SAF® numbering system; by the mid-1980s he was on the SAF® Advisory Board.

Roger had business associates in West Virginia with a very ill horse. Several vets had been consulted and none could come up with a diagnosis. The horse hadn't responded to any treatment and it was obvious to all that the animal was dying. He was to be put out of his misery soon and his owners were devastated.

In conversing with Joe Scogna about this sad circumstance, Joe assured Roger he could discover the ailment of ANY being, human or animal.

"After all," he reasoned, "all living beings possess Life Energy. It is a matter of tapping into that energy field to find the blockages. SAF® can do this."

It sounded fantastic to Roger, so, just before they were scheduled to put the horse down, Roger convinced his friends to give SAF® a try. They were eager to find the disease and take whatever measures were necessary to save the animal. But they didn't want him to suffer any longer.

Joe flew to Pittsburgh in his single engine airplane, with the bulky Life Energy Research Computer System in tow, and then drove with Roger to the elegant home of his friends. It was a BIG spread, fenced and cross-fenced. It was such a large horse ranch that the four of them drove down a long lane to the stable to examine the dying horse.

The original Apple system Joe used was cumbersome, with dual disk drives, interface cords to and from the Infrared Sensitizer, a heavy monitor and keyboard. There wasn't a tower then, no memory to speak of; the many 5.5-inch floppies contained the "memory" of this system.

Finally, finding an electric outlet in the stable and using extension cords, Joe set up the system as Roger regaled his friends about SAF® and its ability to find diseases, hidden obscure diseases that might have been missed.

Truth be told, Joe didn't know anything about this horse or any horse, or if SAF® would even be able to read the energy of the animal. Would the energy translate into symptom patterns as in a human being? But he deftly performed an infrared scan of the horse's head as he had done countless times on humans.

"I've been all around the world with my businesses and have reported on all types of health and self-improvement programs. There is nothing like SAF® anywhere – it's quite miraculous! I am flabbergasted at how my own life has been enriched with my personal SAF® program." - Roger Willoughby-Ray

A series of beeps were heard as the temperature readings fed into his computing system. And an image slowly appeared on the computer screen.

"I was totally embarrassed," Roger stated later. "I was obviously expecting a horse's head to appear on the screen and instead it was the image of a human face, a template! How could I explain this?"

Roger fidgeted as he waited to hear about the disease of this horse. "I could not have anticipated what was to happen next."

A Dying Horse Gets his Wish

SAF® chains are a series of numbers that relate to organs and glands, emotions and conditions. Combinations of these numbers tell the story of syndromes and diseases.

After the infrared scan had been completed, Joe Scogna sort of hesitated when he saw the numbers on the screen, but gave the interpretation as he saw it, not knowing what to expect.

Instead of identifying a disease, Joe said, "He doesn't like his work, right here, a 3-4-5 in the core."

He turned to the three for a response.

The woman answered a bit tersely, "We don't work him - he isn't a workhorse. He's a fine thoroughbred!"

Roger cringed and said later he could feel the blood draining away; he was certain he was white as a sheet. Obviously this trip was a mistake. Joe Scogna didn't know horseflesh.

Undeterred, Joe turned back to the computer screen

and continued. "He's lost his zest for living, this 13-17/18," he pointed to the lead numbers in the sequence on the screen. "And the 13-20 up-link shows he's homesick and depressed. Whatever happened, whatever changes were made, this was all very traumatic for the horse and it has upset his hormone balance," he stated matter-of-factly.

After a brief silence, the weight of his words sunk in; both owners began speaking at once.

"He's a fine racehorse, a Derby champ we purchased at great expense!"

"We wanted to recoup our money by putting him out to stud, but he's impotent!"

"He has the best of everything here, the pasture, the feed, the peace and quiet for his retirement years."

"The best vets, and yet, he's going downhill!"

As the story unfolded, the couple finally understood the messages their horse was sending them. They had taken him from the fast-paced life of the racing circuit where he had been tops in his class, away from that energy and vitality, and had moved him to their bucolic country estate where they planned to recover their investment by using him for breeding purposes. But the horse missed the excitement of his old life and job, wasn't interested in the new life they were providing, which included the willing mares.

"It's right here," said Joe, "the 13-17/18-20 tells us the loss of zest for living, loss of sexual powers. He is depressed about the move and can't perform at his new job, providing offspring."

Mystery solved. The emotional issues beneath the "illness" had been brought to the surface by the SAF® chain, and the owners decided to make some changes. The stallion would receive more attention and grooming from people, uplifting, parade-type music, flags waving and fanfare.

Last I heard, the horse was doing well, interested in

mares, and living up to his potential as a stud.

EVEN knowing only a few numbers, the story image is clear.

Race Horse Case Study (with Infrared)

Chain: 13-17/18-3-4-5-6-20

Lead: 13 (emotionally drained)
Core: 3-4-5 (dislikes work)
Anchor: 20 (location)

Depression; 13-17/18-3-4-5-6-20

Stress Up-Links:
3-4-5: dislikes work

5-6: plans, ideas, wishes being thwarted.

13-17/18: Impotence, loss of zest for living, all but given up hope.

Business Pro: Work stoppage, Work Suppression

Emotion Hazards: feel blamed, feel like a failure, overwhelmed by the environment.

Humans, you can understand the hidden messages of body, mind and spirit with SAF® chain work.

"The insights and connections the infrared reveals continue to astound me even after years of seeing it work.

Following the numerical pattern of a client's chain, generated by the infrared, combined with client history, dialogue and experience, unravels years of stress from the body, mind and spirit.

We can use this incredible technology to gain new awareness and educate ourselves on how to see our own light and untapped potential, and help others do the same." —Sandy Aquila

Omaha Healing Arts Center (OM Center). "The city that starts with a mantra OM and ends in enlightenment Aha!

How can I find out what MY numbers are?

Currently, the two most used methodologies for creating a sequence of numbers are the SAF® Questionnaires (SAF-120; Stress-120 and the Q-24) and Infrared scans, particularly of the face area, done with the Infrared Sensitizer (ExTech IR 200).

At www.LifeEnergyResearch.com, complete the Stress 120 Questionnaire to create a chain, or have an Infrared scan completed to create a chain of numbers.

The questionnaires present a subjective viewpoint of your priorities, that is, your reality as you see it, with probable causes as yet unknown to you.

The special Infrared Sensitizer, available at practitioners' offices, is able to pick up nuances of invisible energy flowing in and around you, translate this into an SAF® sequence of numbers, and present an accurate image of what traumatic events in your past (that are in your subconscious) are affecting your level of awareness in the present.

Then, with a practitioner, you can begin work on your awareness levels. You will find that as the unconscious and shadow side rises to your consciousness, the energy, the stuck energy of the shadow side, will be released.

Unlock the mysteries of your mind

The overall task of the SAF® program is to find the exact sequence of experience that will be the key to unlock the mysteries of confusion, which may be preventing your abilities from coming into full bloom. Abilities such as artistic, musical, mental telepathy, intuition, future seer, distance healing and other long-forgotten abilities. Right now, you must think about that situation or that confusion of energy that is getting in your way; this would be your complaint, what you want to understand. The traumatic event, or the "dragon" presents itself for one specific reason - it dares you to figure it out.

SAF® uses numbers to find out how much power those unknown, unrealized traumas and events exert over you. The challenge is there, but YOU are the main ingredient.

Learn about the theory and the unique numbering system presented in ***SAF Simplified.***

Continue working on your SAF sequences. As the energy of the past unknown, hidden traumas is released, you will finally make the connections, and realize your true native, innate abilities.

Words from Happy Clients!

Holy Cow! I just finished an SAF® session and I feel about 10,000 pounds lighter! Thank you!"

"I have a lot more energy since I've stopped seeing my situation as such a burden."

Through chain work, as I prioritize and balance things in life differently, I find I have more balance within myself."

"I never realized how defensive I was and how I magnetized so many people into my life that were emotional pollutants for me. After my SAF® session, I see them without being defensive, and now I'll just withdraw from them."

"I am now much more aware that my lifetime patterns have been in the genetic pooling. I'm excited that the chains have been broken—these were long-term issues through generations! :)"

What Practitioners say about SAF® Infrared & Online

"I love infrared because it bypasses one's defenses and gets right to the heart of the matter, or the spleen or the colon. It is simple to use and reliable. Everyone who has been scanned is blown away, and wants to know, How could it know that about me?"—Nancy Porter, DN, Iowa.

"SAF® Online is dynamite! Saves hours of time, gets to the core immediately to help resolve traumas and emotional patterns."
—James Manegold, Pennsylvania

"The SAF® Online service is awesome! With the Modality Sorter, I can find if exercise, acupuncture, or yoga is needed. Working with the withholds has been the most dramatic and rewarding for releasing energy."
—Paulline Caraher, Arizona

"I use both SAF® questionnaires and the Infrared. Amazing! With the questionnaires, we have the patient's point of view; however, English is the 2nd or 3rd language for my patients so I use the Infrared more often. It is an interesting tool—scans on babies have been very impressive!"
—Dr. Jim Eerebout, MD, MA Belgium

"SAF online is quick and easy to use, an extremely advanced technology for personal change and for helping others. The Up-Links in the interpretations create a comprehensive picture of the ages when traumas occurred, where in the body they are located and how they are impacting our lives in the present."
—Brian Kilian, Tennessee

Part Two: The Guide to SAF® Online

What it is & How to Use it

- Holistic Evaluations (Questionnaires & Infrared)
- Holistic Solutions (Interpretations & Remedies)
- **Help Clients disconnect from past traumas**

Let Life Energy Research take care of the administration and the paperwork, so you can concentrate on your clients and your own self awareness work.

www.LifeEnergyResearch.com/safonline

What is SAF® Online?

SAF® Online is a subscription service for SAF Practitioners, coaches, students, interested researchers and nutritional enthusiasts. It can be accessed at:
www.LifeEnergyResearch.com/safonline

SAF® Online is a fast and cost effective way to:

- Handle SAF® chain paperwork
- Cut down on research time, especially with difficult symptoms and cases
- Help clients and participants increase their vibration level, their consciousness.
- Help clients and participants disconnect from past traumas.
- Help clients and participants achieve their goals on body, mind and spirit levels with chain sequence work.
- Find a remedy based on the chain. Choose Interpretations and Remedies for chain-owners.
- Give a boost to your business.

SAF® Online has detailed onscreen instructions, but sometimes seeing it in print, and holding the book makes the learning curve easier.

Troubleshooting: Please use Mozilla Firefox. With changing internet and computer technology here and abroad, we are continually making upgrades behind the scenes and have found Internet Explorer and Google Chrome to be less than perfect.

Where does SAF® Online come from?

History: The SAF® Online system presents an almost overwhelming number of options in Interpretations and Remedy selection. These interpretations were written by Joseph R. Scogna, Jr, and programmed by two young men while in high school – geniuses – who have since had stellar careers with Microsoft and HP. In the past, SAF® practitioners purchased the computer equipment and 5 or 10 programs pertinent to their practices. We are again fortunate to have an outstanding programmer to update the old Apple IIe programs – updated and infinitely more readable!

We have included dozens of these programs in SAF® Online. No one is expected to utilize or even understand all of them! You may find 5 or more you work with on a consistent basis. What an acupuncturist finds useful will differ from a health or nutrition coach, a medical doctor, a nurse, a naturopath, a physician's assistant, an herbalist, a massage therapist, a chiropractor, an energy psychologist or a light therapist.

Remember, the point of SAF® work is to help your clients and participants find resolutions to issues and patterns in their life; to increase vibrational level and consciousness, to find a remedy or pinpoint an allergy or sensitivity. You are assisting in this process. Your client doesn't want to be bogged down with too much information any more than you do!

It is hoped that you will experiment with these Interpretations and Remedies and find what works best for you in your practice. See Sample Reports, pages 39, 49, 77-83.

SAF® Online works seamlessly with the online chain

generation formats: Stress 120, SAF-120 and the Q-24 Questionnaires, as well as the ExTech IR200 Infrared device discussed earlier in this book. All questionnaires are free of charge and will create a chain sequence of numbers. Infrared devices are purchased separately and must be used in person.

The SAF® Online service is here for you, the busy practitioner. With this service, practitioners and coaches can get right to the business of deciphering the chains of their clients, find remedies and help with life-style changes.

Do you have a difficult case with confusing symptoms? Have you tried everything and just need a new view? You are in the right spot!

Now, let's get started!

9 EASY Steps for SAF® ONLINE

Chain Data Collection and Interpretations

How SAF® ONLINE can be used by and for You

1. Open an SAF® Online account with LOGIN (your email address) and PASSWORD. If you forget your password, click link for another to be sent to you. Once you get the new one, reset to a password you will remember.
2. Once you are in your account, create a file for yourself, including birth date, and note your CLIENT KEY.
3. Click on Questionnaires, complete a questionnaire. (Stress 120 for emotional symptoms; SAF 120 for physical symptoms; Q-24 for variety and a faster process.) Or, click the button “Enter Infrared Data” and follow the instructions on pages 17-21 this book. Questionnaires and Infrared will create a chain (An infrared device is required for this option).
4. After completing the Questionnaire, use your own CLIENT KEY, click SUBMIT and all data will go to your own file for yourself. You’ll receive an email that a client “has completed a questionnaire”. All the chain data is now available.
5. Go back to your SAF® Online account; find the Client file (your own). Click the chain you want to work with (by date) and it is displayed, with Lead, Core, Anchor and special up-links, if any.
6. On the screen, SELECT INTERPRETATION will allow you to choose a single Interpretation.
7. If you choose one INTERPRETATION, on the

screen, click INSTRUCTIONS for how to use that one Interpretation. Refer also to this THE GUIDE TO SAF® ONLINE for that INTERPRETATION.

8. On the screen, GENERATE REPORT will allow you to choose several Interpretations at once. The Report will be downloaded to your computer, can be saved in your computer files, or printed for your hard copy files.
9. Refer to the INSTRUCTIONS or this THE GUIDE TO SAF® ONLINE for information on each Interpretation and Remedy.

How SAF® ONLINE can be used by you for Clients and Participants

1. Open an SAF® Online account with LOGIN (your email address) and PASSWORD. If you forget your password, click link for another to be sent to you. Once you get the new one, reset to a password you will remember.
2. Once you are in your account, create a file for each client, including the birth date, and note the CLIENT KEY. Let your clients know their own CLIENT KEY so all the SAF® data will be sent to your file for that one client.
3. Instruct your client to complete a questionnaire (Stress 120 for emotional symptoms; SAF® 120 for physical symptoms; Q-24 for variety and a faster process.). Questionnaires and INFRARED scanning, will create a chain sequence (infrared device is required for this option).
4. Instruct your client to SUBMIT their CLIENT KEY at the completion of a Questionnaire, which will allow all data to go to your file for that client. You will receive an email that “a client has completed a questionnaire”. All the chain data is now available.
5. Go to your SAF® Online account, Select the cli-

ent, Click the chain you want to work with by date, and it is displayed, with Lead, Core, Anchor and special up-links, if any.

6. On the screen, SELECT INTERPRETATION will allow for a single interpretation.
7. If you choose one INTERPRETATION, on the screen, click INSTRUCTIONS for how to use that one Interpretation. Refer also to this THE GUIDE TO SAF® ONLINE for that INTERPRETATION.
8. On the screen, click GENERATE REPORT will allow you to choose several Interpretations at once. The Report will be downloaded to your computer, can be saved in your computer files, printed for your hard copy files, or emailed to your client.
9. Refer to the INSTRUCTIONS or this THE GUIDE TO SAF® ONLINE for information on each Interpretation and Remedy.

Special Features for Practitioners & Coaches

- Instructions – On screen, below the title of Interpretation, click the button for instructions to the practitioner regarding that Interpretation. Refer also to this GUIDE.
- Special Up-Links - “depression” and “withhold” will appear below the lead, core, anchor, if applicable to that sequence of numbers.
- Generate Report - choose several Interpretations and Remedy categories at one time.
- Age of Traumas/Events - located in the first column (left) on the Operative Words Chart
- Manual Input – Add a Chain: Chain sequences can be typed in manually from remote sources.

Understanding the Bar Graphs & Single Items

Bar-Graph Format: The top bar graph item reflects the lead of the chain, the effect or the result. The middle items relate to the core; and the bottom bar graphs to the anchor or cause. You may choose the top and the bottom for balance, or just the top for clarity and relief.

Two Line Group Format: one line is shaded. Top line reflects the lead area; bottom line relates to the anchor. Choose one or more from each group for balance.

List of Items Format: Compare these items to the complaint in the homeopathic style, and choose which best fits the client's issues and or complaint.

Interpretations & Remedies

Sample reports follow the section on Interpretations and Remedies and can be reviewed for furthering your understanding of the SAF® Online system.

SAF® Operative Words 1-6, with Ages This Operative Chart is used for emotional release work as presented in SAF® Training Course material. Find age of traumas and events (only appears when the complete birth date of the client is used) and the emotion words to discuss for the resolution of patterns.

Stress Up-Links These are syndromes, as presented in *SAF® Simplified*; SAF® Road Map Training, Level 1 Course material.

SAF® Operative Words 1-6, with Ages Use this evaluation for SAF®-120 Questionnaires for physical symptoms. Find the present disturbance and what in the past may have caused it. The age is found in the first column. SAF® Training, Level 2.

SAF® Up-Links These are syndromes as presented in *SAF® Simplified* and SAF® Training, Level 2 Course material.

Acu-Track (Bar-Graph Format) includes the acupuncture-acupressure points/meridians that require evaluation in order to bring about balance for the client. Use these items as trained in that discipline along with acupressure / acupuncture charts.

Combinations of SAF® organs and glands in the chain reveal pressure (buildup of stuck energy) and space (energy flows too quickly), and thus SAF® aligns Western medicine with Eastern philosophies and medicine (TCM and TAM). On the bar graphed list, the pressurized meridians are located at the top of the list, while those with less pressure can be found at the bottom.

Refer to *SAF® Modality Sorter, SAF® Simplified* and SAF® Training Level 2.

Alchem-184 (List of Items Format) contains single formula Homeopathic remedies, with Common and Latin names. Once the chain has revealed the items, cross-verify with symptom listings in a homeopathic text as trained in that discipline.

Companion books for reference: *Homeopathic Self Appraisal Index* (all remedies listed) and *Homeopathy Revisited* are excellent resources; SAF® Training Level 2.

Amino Acids (Bar-Graph Format) is used for a mental assist in SAF® work and to find nutritional deficiencies. Amino Acids are the building blocks of protein; the DNA in the protein structure of organs and glands contain the recordings of lifetime events. In this capacity of emotional release work, SAF® uses Amino Acids to assist the client in clarifying mental images. Use Remedy Red glandulars for locating images and Amino Acids to sharpen the images.

Companion reference book: *Amino Acids - A Nutritional Guide*, and SAF® Training, Level 2.

Antidote-1 (List of Items Format) is used when the client has been running many chains, or participating in so many different health or awareness methods and desperately seeking remedies to help retrieve mental images and memories, that sometimes this needs to be calmed down.

Refer to: *SAF® Modality Sorter, Junk DNA: Unlocking the Hidden Secrets of Your DNA.*

Business Pro (Bar-Graph Format) is especially helpful in today's troubled times. This Interpretation is NOT for executives only because we all participate in the business of life. We mirror our personal issues and symptoms in the workplace and "bring our work home" — business and personal life are often synonymous. Are you in a stress management position at work? Do you know anyone with business troubles?

The top items relate to the lead and the present time, a result of the pattern. The middle items refer to the core; and the bottom bar graphs to the anchor or cause. All items are important, however, address the top items with the longest bar graph first; ask your client,

"What does _______ mean to you?

Chinese Herbs (5 Groups) (Bar-Graph Format) will be easily understood by those schooled in TCM, TAM, or Ayurvedic medicinal approaches, along with SAF®, where helping the client find balance is the key. Where there is yin/yang balance, there is harmony and health.

The names may have changed when these herbs found their way West in British homeopathic and herbal formulations, and as trade has opened further with China. Chinese herbals generally suggest if the body is cold, heat it with Hot or Warm herbs; if the body is hot, cool it with Chilly or Mildly Chilly herbs. Some herbs match more subtle natures, such as the Bland items.

Let these 5 Interpretations find the best balance! Based on the metabolic doubles in the chain, herbs from the proper group will appear – **Bland, Chilly**, **Hot, Mildly Chilly** or **Warm**.

Herbs can be ordered through Chinese Herbs Direct.

Color Coordinator, (Bar-Graph Format) with its 24 different hues is especially helpful for light therapists, Feng shui, jewelry, mental imaging and meditation, and other techniques that utilize color for balance. These are not the "chakra" colors but instead follow the precepts of Eastern 5 Element Theory. There is not one stock color that will bring about balance for everyone, every time. In SAF® we understand this - each of us is unique and each chain is a reflection of our uniqueness.

When we are healthy, we naturally take in the colors we need. Use pairs of colors to achieve balance and harmony in the chain sequence and with the client.

Order bead strands of appropriate type and color from www.kyaniteking.com.

Culinary Herbs (Two Line Group Format), when cut fresh from the garden or purchased locally, the stronger their intrinsic value. These herbs can be used as part of the daily juicing, cooking or raw food routine. Choose one or several from each group for the best effect.

Each of these suggestions is Client-specific (chain-specific) for that personal touch. With SAF® release work, you are addressing the stressed organs and glands and with these herbs are helping to harmonize the energy of the client and increase the vibration level.

Delete Drugs (Bar-Graph Format) is used when drug materials (antibiotics, stimulants, narcotics, OTCs, hormones, regulators, etc.), which are frequencies incompatible with human energy, are interfering with mental processing. There may be powerful residues in the body that are now creating new symptoms and reactions, electrical charges, distortion of memory images, hallucinations, or no confidence that energy of the major complaint has been rectified. A detoxification is needed.

Consider: Millennium Detox Interpretation. Consult: *SAF® Modality Sorter, SAF® Simplified, The Threat of the Poison Reign, Junk DNA: Unlocking the Hidden Secrets of Your DNA*, SAF® Training, Level 2.

Emotion Hazards (Bar-Graph Format) is particularly good for addictions counseling, the new energy medicine, EFT, bio-energetic healers, myofascial and emotional release. The biggest obstacle to awareness is often the unseen and unrecognized patterns of behavior, self-defeating thoughts. Here you'll find what hazards may trip up the client and trigger reactions. These are Client-specific, based on the numbers in the chain sequence. All items are important, however, address the items with the longest bar graphs first; ask your client, "What does ____ mean to you?"

This interpretation can open the case! How does SAF® do this? The problem situation was always within the client: with SAF® techniques, the answer can be found there, too.

Environmentals (Bar-Graph Format) appears on SAF® sorters when various energies in the environment of the client may cause a distraction or electrical interaction with chain sequences being worked. The client must determine the significance of the items; further processing will serve to de-sensitize the electrical energies in the client's environment.

To understand how such distracting energies relate to the human system and cause symptoms and reactions, refer to: *The Promethion, The Threat of the Poison Reign, Junk DNA: Unlocking the Hidden Secrets of Your DNA,* and *SAF® Simplified.*

Consider also Millennium Detox Interpretation, Omni-Track Interpretation, SAF® Training, Level 2.

Essential Oils (Two Line Group Format). Choose one or more from each group listed for a custom blend. Create Client-specific body creams, give unique "drop-type" massages, or make bath salts. Using SAF® Online will give you a clear advantage your clients will appreciate - helping with both emotional release and chain balancing.

Order Essential oils through Amrita Essential Oils: high quality and an excellent value.

Healer's Rescue-1 (List of Items Format) can be used for all those who "touch" clients in their line of work (massage therapists, energy workers, chiropractors), however it is also appropriate for those who practice "distance healing". SAF® has not forgotten about our healers!

Healer's Rescue useful when 15-17/18 appears in a sequence, and when electrical energy from others seems to be interfering with the healer's own energy. The healer must determine the significance of the items.

Continuing SAF® processing (making connections to the past and the major complaint) will serve to de-sensitize the electrical energies and frequencies of these items.

Consult: *SAF® Simplified.* Continue with chain work to prioritize issues in life and learn to spot when interfering energies of another have entered the personal space.

Herbal Treatment (Teas) (Bar-Graph Format) is for Master Herbalists and Naturopaths, those skilled in herbal science. The medicinal effects presented are calculated from the up-links in the SAF® chain and will best help to bring about balance.

Cross-reference the items with symptomatology in herbal texts; create tinctures, capsules, hydrotherapy uses, teas, and compresses, etc. as trained in your profession.

Herb CR08 (Bar-Graph Format) presents herbal items based on the combinations of numbers (the organs and glands) in the chain. Follow the bar graph and add those herbs daily in supplements, juicing, cooking or raw food routines to help bring about balance to the chain and the client.

Herb Scan 46 (Bar-Graph Format) lists common herbal items that can be used as tinctures, in capsule form, as a tea or for bath soaking. These special herbs are generated by the up-links in the chain; the stressed organs and glands are trying to communicate a problem to your client. Those herbs with the longest bar graphs are suggested first.

Juice (Bar-Graph Format) omits the guesswork when recommending specific juices for juice devotees, clients or store customers. Based on the stressed organs and glands in the chain, the juice items with the longest bar graphs would be used first, either by themselves, or added to a green (alkaline) smoothie - a fresh idea sure to revitalize your life or your business. For health food stores, juice bars and personal juicing.

Use either an emulsifier-type juicer to include the fiber or an extractor-type, which separates the juice from the fiber. Both are used commercially.

Mass-Energy Imbalance (Bar-Graph Format) appears because organ/gland combinations in the chain suggest an assist with achieving balance in life is needed.

The client must determine the significance of the items. Continuing with SAF® mental processing and making connections to the past and the major complaint will serve to de-sensitize the electrical energies and frequencies of these items.

Consult: *SAF® Modality Sorter, SAF® Simplified, The Promethion* and *Project Isis: Fundamentals of Human Electricity*. SAF® Training, Level 2.

Metabolic Triples (Special Format). Communication exists within the chain as organ and gland systems balance negative and positive states (needs and abundances). The metabolic triples display the triple point function of electroplasmic entities and the manifestation of symptoms in the third dimension, as explained in SAF® Training, Level 2. This is the SAF® way of saying the client has major physical symptoms in the present time that are pressing in on him or her.

This Interpretation is essential for SAF® 120 Questionnaires for physical symptoms.

Consult: *The Promethion; Junk DNA: Unlocking the Hidden Secrets of Your DNA;* SAF® Training, Level 2, TIP (The Metabolic Triple).

Metagenics Master File (List of Items Format) contains products sold by Metagenics and only practitioners can order these through that company. The items are derived from the chain combinations of stressed organs and glands plus emotional issues. Cross-reference items to symptomatology and major complaint.

Millennium Detox (List of Items Format) displays items with frequencies to which the client may be reactive and sensitive (salt, crystals, cleaning soaps, viruses, ELFs, polluted water, etc). The client must determine the significance of the items. Continuing SAF® processing, making connections to the past and the major complaint, will serve to de-sensitize the electrical energies and frequencies of these items.

Consider also: Remedy Orange Interpretation, Omni-Track.

Refer to: *The Threat of the Poison Reign, Remedy Orange, Junk DNA: Unlocking the Hidden Secrets of Your DNA*, and SAF® Training, Level 2.

Modality Sorter (Bar-Graph Format) provides more direction on the chain. Its 69 suggestions are helpful ideas for the client to follow in daily life (acupressure, writing, minerals, stretching, yoga, chiropractic, sound therapy, dental repair, take a walk, etc).

All are important to the chain sequence; however, address those with the longest bar graph first: "What does ____________mean to you?" or "Have you tried ____ lately?"

Consider also: Whatever categories the Modality Sorter suggests, access those Interpretations. Read: *SAF® Modality Sorter* for details.

Mood (Bar-Graph Format) items consist of flower

essences (many are Bach Flower Essences) and homeopathic remedies readily available at local health food and other stores. SAF® takes the guesswork out of selecting these items for the client.

For the greatest effect in energetic balancing, we use the pairs of essences shown by the longest bar graphs. These can be consumed as single remedies under the tongue, by alternating remedies morning and night, or by depositing drops of several remedies in a glass of water and sipping throughout the day.

Read: SAF Training, Level 2, *SAF® KEY and Reference Guide (2009), Organs and Glands: Connections and Breaks*, and the SAF® TIPs in the SAF® Training Manual.

Omni-Track (List of Items Format) displays the items with frequencies in the chain sequence that are being stimulated and need attention. Perhaps this is a high stimulation situation, in what is described in *Junk DNA: Unlocking the Hidden Secrets of your DNA* as a Z reaction. In this case, reactions are hyper-sensitivities or allergies that serve to make the client weaker and less aware of the present circumstances.

These items include 128 sensory perceptions. Once found, the chain-owner can read about these in *Junk DNA: Unlocking the Hidden Secrets of your DNA* for greater understanding.

The client must determine the significance of the items. Continuing SAF® processing, making connections to the past and the major complaint, meditating or journaling thoughts and occurrences will serve to desensitize the electrical energies and frequencies of these items.

Consult: *Junk DNA: Unlocking the Hidden Secrets of your DNA*

Problems, Worries, Upsets (Bar-Graph Format) is used when there are troubles and distracting situations around the client making it extremely difficult to accomplish anything - with chains or in life. The problems have enough electrical charge that the magnetic influence is disrupted. (car, money, being yelled at, family, being wrong, etc.)

The client must determine the significance of each item. Continuing SAF® emotional release work, mental processing, and making connections to the past and to the major complaint will serve to de-sensitize the electrical energies and frequencies of these items.

Consult: *SAF® Simplified* and continue with chain work to learn to prioritize issues. SAF® Road Map Level 1 Training.

Remedy Blue 82 (List of Items Format) contains homeopathic combination remedies (light polarizers). Symptoms are listed for each item number – compare to client's symptoms, their complaint and the chain; recommend the appropriate items.

Remedy Blue is used for correcting symptoms in a homeopathic manner and for SAF® mental assists - in both cases, the products turn down the volume or turn off the mental image pictures altogether, which in time allows the client to confront images and mental situations better.

Consult: *SAF® Modality Sorter.* Companion books: *Homeopathy Revisited, Homeopathy Self-Appraisal Index,* SAF® Training, Level 2.

Remedy Orange (Bar-Graph Format) contains suggestions of homeopathic antigens to which the client is reactive or sensitive. Standard medical protocols may find the client has NO allergies, and yet energies and electrical frequencies are building up to a fever pitch.

The client with allergies or sensitivities cannot control buildups of mass and energy patterns on certain wavelengths and frequencies; there may be an overload. The person may be creating situations within his own mind and spirit that are too much to cope with at present.

The client must determine the significance of the items. SAF® processing, making connections to the past and the major complaint, will serve to de-sensitize the electrical energies and frequencies of these items.

Companion books: *Remedy Orange* to cross-reference the symptomatology presented.

Refer to: *SAF® Modality Sorter, Junk DNA: Unlocking the Hidden Secrets of Your DNA*, Millennium Detox Interpretation, SAF® Training, Level 2.

Remedy Red Expanded (Two Line Group Format) is necessary when the client cannot see mental image pictures (memories), or even find them. The organs and glands as taught in SAF® contain the entire history of the traumatic situations and all genetic material of incidents that have occurred in the past.

Glands are light based (sun-generated) so use of homeopathic glandular preparations and light polarization techniques are possible for expanding the energy in and around the gland and thus freeing up the images.

Refer to: *Interview with Joe Scogna, 1982; Junk DNA: Unlocking the Hidden Secrets of your DNA*

Companion books: *SAF® Modality Sorter, SAF® Simplified, Homeopathy Revisited*, and *Amino Acids - a Nutritional Guide*. SAF® Training, Level 2.

Run Escape (Bar-Graph Format) is useful when the client has reached the end of his or her rope! At some point, client's ability to survive well has been quashed or torn asunder by circumstances. When escape is not an option, when desperation reigns, when the client needs to be energized and validated, Run Escape will help to bring forth the essential balance and put life on an even keel.

The client must determine the significance of each item. Ask the client: "What does _____ mean to you?"

Mental processing, journaling, and further chain sequence work will serve to de-sensitize the electrical energies and frequencies that stimulated these items.

Consult: *SAF® Modality Sorter, SAF® Simplified*, SAF® Road Map Level 1 Training, SAF® Training, Level 2.

Vita-Coordinator (Bar-Graph Format) presents a coordinated list of vitamins, minerals and other health related items, based on components of stressed organs and glands plus emotional issues in the chain.

Nutritional, elemental items are depleted from the body through stress, disease, age, radiant energies, and improper diet or digestion. There may be deficiencies (space) or a buildup of toxicities (pressure), both of which hinder health and energy.

We must have the right kind of nutrition and energy to electrify the system so that mental imagery will turn on and be brought forth to be worked upon. When we are fully healthy, we naturally gravitate toward those items we need; we are able to take in what we need from our foods, surroundings, and other input sources.

This interpretation takes the guesswork out of the equation. Based on orthomolecular work, hair analysis, pH of urine and saliva, and other research and nutritional protocols, Vita-Coordinator lists the ratios and combinations of certain minerals and other food type items to include, all based on the latest chain of numbers.

Refer to: *The Promethion; SAF® Modality Sorter; The*

Threat of the Poison Reign; Junk DNA: Unlocking the Hidden Secrets of your DNA; SAF® Training, Level 2.

On the following pages, sample chains and printouts are presented. These can be reviewed and compared with the Interpretations and Remedies that have just been discussed. These analyses do not take the place of training and the reader should not assume a complete knowledge of the SAF® method by this one book alone.

Much of the configuring work has been done for the practitioner in this Online system, and with training it becomes an easier process, but there is a depth to this Life Energy work that is augmented and enhanced by the knowledge a practitioner brings to the table through SAF® training, and in his or her own area of expertise.

"I feel so privileged to have had the opportunity of working with the SAF® system of knowledge for the past 25 years.

Art is the language of symbol and of our deep feelings, just as the language of our mind is words. Healing art allows the language of our deep feelings to be heard by the mind. ART becomes the translator for what the SAF® system helps us find.

Recent SAF® work with a client was absolutely astounding! It was like a symbiotic artistic dance that took place between us that facilitated an extraordinary work of art! As the collage formed, it was further documented by the client's powerful words, so descriptive and completely exactly what was envisioned. The layers of the collage came together almost like a holographic process."

—Aurora Karuna

A Quick Look at the Self Awareness Formulas (SAF®):

- Our chain sequence tells a tale of organ and gland systems, with correlating emotions and conditions. These are connected through time; the ages help us focus and remember what we need to.
- Using SAF®, we can learn about our patterns - physical, emotional, and spiritual.
- SAF® can radiate energy into the unconscious to make it conscious.
- When the past is in perspective, the present becomes synchronized.
- SAF® sheds light into the darkness so we can see.
- SAF® starts the derailing process of unwanted emotional and symptom patterns.
- The hidden program or code is held in the anchor. This helped us survive as helpless children but may be detrimental to us now as adults.
- The culprit may be only one invisible energy.
- A chain contains "chains of information."
- We can dissolve old behavioral and emotional patterns.
- Drugs....of any sort....put a drag on our energy.
- SAF® dissects problems into finer and smaller particles so we can understand them.
- Time does not heal all wounds.
- Unresolved traumas are alive & take our energy.

"We can truthfully say that any person who has spent time on the SAF® program reports great benefits in their life that seem to be structural and long lasting. This is because long-repressed traumas and patterns of behavior have been exposed through the symptom awareness process. Also, they realize that they are the ones who make the connections and the necessary changes.

— Tim McCarthy, Clinic Program Director

Sample Reports

Created from Questionnaire: SAF 120

Name: Mr. Chin
age: 44
Complaint: can't sleep
stress #: 180
Chain: 12-13-1-19-2-5-10-17/18-20-16-21
Lead: 12
Core: 5
Anchor: 21

Depression: 13-1-19-2-5-10-17/18-20

Stress Up-Links

12-13: Projects and plans left undone cause insomnia; need REM sleep; electric pressures built up, need to be discharged.
1-19: Losing border integrity; heat, pain, redness, swelling
10-17/18: overweight; fat deposits (insulation) protect from intolerable stress but bad for body
16-21: kidney stones (poisons in system start to solidify).

Acu-Track

—————————— B-23 Shen Yu
——————– Li-10 Shou San Li
—— Gv-26 Shui Kou
—- Gb-2 Ting Hui
————— Tsuan Chu B-2
—————————— Th-3 Chung Chu

Modality Sorter

—————————— Thought Processes (Memory)
—————————— Rest and Sleep
—————— Activity
—— Chiropractic (TMJ)
—— Meditation (Electric Discharge)
—————— Tranquilization
—————————— Muscle Resistance (Kinesiology)
—————————— Homeopathy

Created from Questionnaire: Stress-120

Name: Carol
Age: 27
Complaint: upset with mother
Stress #: 234
Chain: 13-16-1-12-20-2-9-5-23-4-7-11
Lead: 13
Core: 2-9
Anchor: 11
Withhold: 1-12-20-2-9
Depression: 13-16-1-12-20

Operative Words 1-6

Age	#	Organ/Gland	Action	Condition	Emotion	Low Emotion	High Emotion
26.4 - present	13	adrenal glands	pressure	capacitance	courage	shame	pride
24 - 26.4	16	kidneys	refuse	filtration	fear	poisoned	purify
21.6 - 24	1	thymus	against	protection	aggression	reaction	action
19.2 - 21.6	12	brain/nervous system	time	electricity	nervous	complicated	simplify
16.8 - 19.2	20	pancreas/solar plexus	quality	location	laughter	suppressed	express
14.4 - 16.8	2	heart	run	synchronization	love	deny	accept
12 - 14.4	9	bones/muscles	hold	locomotion	pain	blamed	respond
9.6 - 12	5	anterior pituitary	direct	coordination	observant	controlled	master
7.2 - 9.6	23	spleen	do	rejection	antagonize	regret	appreciate
4.8 - 7.2	4	stomach	dissolve	digestion	happy	eaten	assimilate
2.4 - 4.8	7	lungs	exchange	vaporization	monotony	stifled	refresh
birth - 2.4	11	veins/arteries	move	circulation	resentment	gravity	games

Stress Up-Links

13-16: failed a test of strength or courage, turned away from danger; phobia about future plans and projects; stuck in a rut

Color Coordinator

————Red/Red Violet
————Violet

Essential Oils

nutmeg, myrrh, grapefruit, rosemary, thyme, basil, clary sage, lemon grass, balsam fir

helichrysum, orange, grapefruit, bergamot, rosemary, basil, clary sage, spruce

Created from Questionnaire: Q-24

Name: Jon
age: 55
Complaint: overwhelmed by life issues
Stress #: 125
Chain: 20-23-6-9-10-2-15-1-21-12-13-7-5
Lead: 20
Core: 15
Anchor: 5

Stress Up-Links
12-13: Projects and plans left undone cause insomnia, need REM sleep; electric pressures built up, need to be discharged.

Metabolic Triples
Disturbance in the spleen (allergies),
causing disturbances of the pancreas-solar plexus (hypoglycemia),
due to liver or gall bladder upset, dysfunction.

Millennium Detox
Polluted Water
Rickettsia
Soaps/Cleaning Fluids
Yeasts And Fungi
Heavy Metals
Salt
Tetracycline
Long Term Viruses
Crystals/Jewelry

Mood
——————— Sweet Chestnut
————— Oak
———— Poison Nut
—— Mimulus
— Olive
—— Hornbeam
———— Mustard
————— Centuary
——————— Agrimony

Created from an Infrared Scan

Name: Jim
Age: 31
Complaint: Painful Wrist
Chain: 15-17/18-1-20-9-12-14-3-4-6-10-11
Lead: 15
Core: 12-14
Anchor: 11

Withhold: 1-20-9

Stress Up-Links:
15-17/18: "Healer's syndrome", absorbing energy of another, picking up reminders from others
1-20: frustration of energy not completed, thwarted; electrical friction (completing, not completed); temptation; sexual perversity causes acid-basic imbalance, ulcerations, sores
4-6: civilization disease (indigestion), gas, rumbling, biliousness
10-11: inability to put plans and dreams into action, peculiar upsets blocking ability to be creative

Omni-Track:
Tone of Sound
Unconscious Sensation
Death from Sensation
The Color Green
The Sound So
Winning
Controlled Personal Motion
Magnetic Position
Protein—Internal

Created from an Infrared Scan

Name: Sarah
Age: 71
Complaint: Heart issues
Chain: 12-10-13-6-15-20-8-11-22-9-23-14
Lead: 12
Core: 20-8
Anchor: 14

Depression: 13-6-15-20

Stress Up-Links:
10-13: malabsorption, trouble with diet
8-11: creating physical problems from mental worries, varicose veins, hemorrhoids, need to detoxify

Amino Acids:
———— Lysine
—— Glutamic Acid
—— Arginine
———— Serine

Juice
—————— Parsley
———— Carrot
— Jerusalem Artichoke
— Endive
———— Celery
—————— Spinach

Created from an Infrared Scan, with Explanations

Client: 52 year old woman
Complaint: tired and exhausted
The chain: 8-3-19-9-4-6-10-15-24-12-14-17/18

Core: 6-10: The chain is telling us about anxiety and sadness.
She confirmed she felt this, but insisted she thought it was a separate issue, not related to her complaint.

Lead: 8: Sex organs, apathy.
She said she was separated, was no longer sexually active, wasn't being creative either, so this made sense.

Anchor: 17/18: Endocrine system is out of balance, hormones are upset.
She agreed; she said she was menopausal, which had altered her world considerably. Her life was out of balance!

Up-Links (the syndromes)
4-6: indigestion, gas, rumbling.
She said she did have colon issues (#3), and was trying to resolve the gas and indigestion with her doctor.

15-24: drug experiences have affected sense perception.
At first she denied using drugs, but when it was explained that even over the counter "medicines" and all prescriptions are considered drugs in SAF work, she understood. She decided to work on the colon issues nutritionally with alkalizing juices and herbs instead. She promised to read the Physician's Desk Reference on the side effects of the drugs she was consuming.

14-17/18: general business troubles, building up of fat cells for protection.
This link made a lot of sense to her. She was always dieting and working out; and was worried about her income ever since retiring.

Business Pro: Work Stoppage.
She laughed. She had taken early retirement. Out of boredom,

she was volunteering at a food kitchen but really missed the daily excitement at her old job.

As she reviewed the events in her recent life, she realized the emotions anxiety and sadness were definitely a part of the present time complaint. All the Up-Links, the chain, and Business Pro rang true. She was amazed.

She had expected, even wanted (!) the chain to be about something else—a long, drawn-out argument with friends—but now understood it was a snapshot of her world, not about her friends, but about her reactions to those exchanges.

She happily stated she could only change herself.

This is what can be done with emotional release work using SAF®. With very little directing other than the emotion words presented to her, those emotional clues to follow, the client made the connections herself.

There was a clear shift of energy as she had an attitude change.

This is how we can help our clients, as facilitators to the process.

"Years ago, I began studying SAF® and am so glad it is back in my life! It has helped me focus on what I want to create for me, and now I'm doing the same for others.

In one case, the client related to the up-link 10-15 as an artist's block and vowed to get back into her painting, which had given her immense joy but she had put it all away.

In another, as the client counted the years back to the trauma, she yelped, "No freaking way!! I thought I was past all that!" I explained that sometimes we leave an emotional component behind, to be realigned. How gratifying; she was finally able to put another piece to rest.

I love the infrared! I work with SAF® Online almost every day, to find Homeopathics and Bach Remedies."

—Kathy Jerore, ND, SAF Practitioner

References and Further Reading www.KathyScogna.com

The following Books and Courses were mentioned in this manual; each will further explain, educate and enhance the Self Awareness Formulas experience for practitioners and participants.

Amino Acids, a Nutritional Guide

History and use in SAF® work for mental clarity and for correcting deficiencies. Homeopathic preferred (light polarizers expand energy).

Homeopathic Self Appraisal Index

184 homeopathic remedies of herbs and other substances, history and use with Alchem-184 Interpretation. All ingredients listed, also found in Remedy Blue products. ISBN: 978-1503275423

Homeopathy Revisited: A Modern Energetic View of an Ancient Healing Art ISBN: 978-1499536706

The history of homeopathy and our science of energy, with questionnaire, book evaluation and find a remedy.

Interview with Joe Scogna (see below)

Scogna's early studies in radiation and electromagnetic principles. (a Kindle e-Book, Amazon)

SAF® Modality Sorter (see below)

69 different therapies and helpful activities to bal-

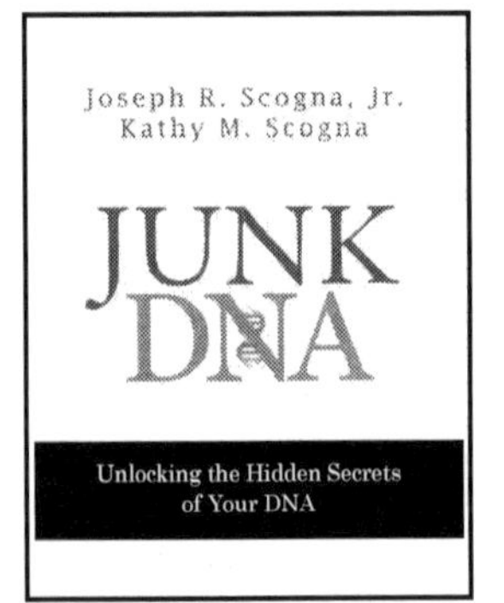

Getting started with SAF®
Three must-have books for the library:

The Promethion: A Comprehensive Study of the Principles of Life Energy. Every researcher needs this, but especially with SAF® work. Scogna reunites spiritual alchemy with physical alchemy; the elements are viewed from an energetic stance. How to balance the electric pressure levels with its pair, with color, touch, nutrients, herbs, and more. This is the background work (physics).

SAF Simplified: Self Awareness Formulas. Organs and glands and dragons, simplified! Theory, numbers, emotions to help the reader get started on emotional release work.

The Threat of the Poison Reign: A Treatise on Electromagnetic Pollution: Radiation and radiant energies—what are these, what can we do? Radiation Cocktail of nutrients. Use with SAF Online: Millennium Detox, Remedy Red, Vita-Coordinator. As a result of his radiation studies, Joe Scogna developed the SAF numbering system. This book started it all!

ance and enhance SAF® chain work.

Project Isis: Fundamentals of Human Electricity ISBN: 978-1500195380

Life Energy and Human Electricity! How we create power and energy, mental image pictures and the effects of mass-energy imbalance (see more on page 40).

Remedy Orange: Allergy Symptoms and Nutritional Support

Explains the allergens found with Remedy Orange Interpretation, plus what foods to add or delete for support and balance.

SAF® Simplified: Self Awareness Formulas

The definitive work, see pages 53 and 85.

Junk DNA: Unlocking the Hidden Secrets of Your DNA (see page 84) ISBN: 978-1502336613

5 senses? How about 128 sensory channels we can use to sense our world. Paradigm-shifting for self awareness, energetic work and all humankind on Earth. Includes DNA inscriptions from the beginning of life in this planetary sector, crystals and the 16 steps of the Z Process, which aligns both creation and evolution. A must-have book; start your journey to Self Awareness!

The Promethion: A Comprehensive Study of the Principles of Life Energy ISBN: 0-9652292-6-2

The Periodic Table of Elements and how to achieve balance. (see more on pages 8 and 85)

The Threat of the Poison Reign: A Treatise on Electromagnetic Pollution

(see more on page 85)

SAF® Road Map, Level 1 Training & Certification

Includes *SAF Simplified*, *Nutrionics*, *Stress Key*,

flashcards, 60 page workbook and check-sheet for correspondence course. Includes 5 hours with SAF® practitioner (by phone) and free time with SAF® Online.

SAF® Training, Level 2 & Certification

Prerequisite: SAF Road Map, Level 1.

Includes *SAF Key & Reference Guide; Organs and Glands-Connections and Breaks;* SAF® Training Manual (165 pages of TIPs and background from seminars, historical data) with workbook and check-sheet for correspondence course. Course includes *The Promethion, The Threat of the Poison Reign* and *Junk DNA: Unlocking the Hidden Secrets of Your DNA*, to be purchased separately. Includes free time with SAF® Online.

Essentials for the Up-to-Date & Knowledgeable SAF® Practitioner!

In order to successfully use Infrared and the Questionnaires in the SAF® protocols, the following are essential:

- *SAF Simplified: Self Awareness Formulas*
- *The SAF® Infrared Manual* (this volume).
- The Extech IR200, the recommended Infrared thermometer for Self Awareness Formulas (SAF®) protocols. (Purchase separately at Amazon)
- SAF Online account, a cost effective subscription service, with Interpretations and Remedies to satisfy many types of practitioner.
- Successful completion of *SAF® Road Map, Level I Training,* with Certificate
- Successful completion of *SAF® Level 2 Training*, with Certificate

Index

Rudolph Ballentine, MD:

"Perhaps the most sophisticated and highly evolved system is that originated by Joseph Scogna. Based on the intensity of flow to twenty-three specific areas, computerized correlations and corresponding sets of organs and mental and emotional traits yields a complex personality inventory. I was impressed by the profound insights into the relationship between my own bodily functions and the psychological and emotional issues that emerged." from *Radical Healing*, page 586, Random House

Louise Hay, Hay House Publishing:

"This system will blow your mind! It is light years ahead of any other form of therapy, and I highly recommend it to anyone who really wants to release old patterns."

Lyn Doole, Colour Light Therapy:

"The more I learn of Quantum Touch, Kinesiology, Chinese Medicine, the work of Walter Russell, and all the Light and Sound and Energy therapies, the more I appreciate how brilliant Joe Scogna was because I see such a synthesis of ideas and modalities in his work.

Dr. Zenea Richler, Academy of Bio-Energetic:

"People on the SAF program are understanding and realizing their own potential. Doing the program has helped my clients (1) to be more aware of how their thoughts are affecting their health, (2) to understand how the environment and other people affect them, and (3) to see new opportunities and new ways to create happier lives for themselves."

Dr. Taucci, MD:

"SAF® work is the greatest! It really is the answer because it incorporates the entire person, body, mind and spirit. The program cuts through to the core and the solution is apparent."

Nic Scogna, SAF Practitioner:

"Finally, with the latest Infrared device, the original breakthrough technology of Joe Scogna has been brought into use again! Now I can collect chain data at expos, shows, and with clients at appointments. The information can be entered on my phone and I can give Lead Core and Anchor information on the spot!

This is instant relief for my clients. The in-depth sessions that follow are so very enlightening and helpful to them."

www.LifeEnergyResearch.com

Made in the USA
Columbia, SC
05 October 2020

22067861R00054